MW00638875

SAVING YOU IS KILLING ME:

LOVING SOMEONE WITH AN ADDICTION

How the Courage to Focus on **You**
Can Help Put Your Life Back Together

ANDREA SEYDEL

Copyright © 2023 by Andrea Seydel

All rights reserved.

Published and distributed in Canada by Live Life Happy Publishing.
www.livelifehappypublishing.com

Library of Congress Cataloging-in-Publication Data
Seydel, Andrea
Saving You Is Killing Me: Loving Someone with An Addiction
Andrea Seydel
1. Nonfiction-Self-help-addiction -2. Non-Fiction-Psychology-Mental Health
ISBN- 978-1-9991409-3-9
First Printing: February 2021. Printed in Canada.
Second Revised Edition: January 2023. Printed in Canada.

Cover Photo Credit: Jeremy Bishop (Underwater)
Proofreader: Lindy Bailey & Linda Bertha Moskovics

Publisher's Note & Author DISCLAIMER

This publication is designed to provide accurate and authoritative information concerning the subject matter covered. It is sold with the understanding that the publisher and author are not engaging in or rendering any psychological, medical or other professional services. If expert assistance or counselling is needed, seek the services of a competent medical professional. For immediate support, call your local crisis line.

ACKNOWLEDGMENTS:

My journey has been a considerable challenge and a profound learning experience, full of shame, heartache and vulnerability. Typically, I would acknowledge the person who inspired the book's creation, but I felt it more fitting to recognize my strength, courage, and loving nature. Going through the turmoil of watching someone you love destroys themselves is heartbreaking, along with all the unacceptable behaviour that comes with loving someone with an addiction.

One of the bravest things I have done is live through and endure this experience. to recover and love me through the process, coming out the outside more resilient than ever.

The plot twist was profoundly hard on me, and nothing is more courageous than admitting you are hurting and struggling. Hidden in the aftermath of the turmoil of loving someone with an addiction, rising from the devastation has been a journey of resilience, growth and discovery for me. What I learned about myself is that:

I can deeply love another person. I am worthy of a healthy relationship. My resourcefulness and ability to bounce back from adversity are profound. People around me are amazingly supportive and loving. From pain and hardship, meaning and purpose can blossom. New possibilities and opportunities are available, and I can now serve others.

I want to acknowledge the authors and researchers referenced in this book. Thank you for all you have taught me about well-being and positive psychology. Whether you realize it or not, your astute knowledge and wisdom have supported me. My success and ability to be resilient are at least in part due to your teaching. I express my deepest gratitude for all your hard work and the knowledge you share with the world. You have inspired me to support others in a way that makes a difference. I truly appreciate and value everything I have learned from you, and I know others will also benefit from your teaching. Your wisdom and support have been invaluable!

Finally, I want to acknowledge you, the reader. I want you to know I see you. I know your pain and have shared this experience, and you are not alone. I've come out the other side, and I want to remind you just how resilient, loving, and courageous you are for purchasing this book and deciding it's time to safeguard your well-being and reclaim a joyful life of happiness.

Sending hugs,
Andrea

"Vulnerability is not winning or losing. It's having the courage to show up for yourself even when you can't control the outcome."

— *Brene Brown*

Contents

"*Happiness stems from loving ourselves and our lives exactly as they are, knowing that joy and pain, strength and weakness, glory and failure are all essential to the full human experience.*"

— *Dr. Kristin Neff*

INTRODUCTION:

Welcome to SYKM! The acronym for Saving You Is Killing Me- Where the struggle of loving someone with an addiction meets the science of human flourishing. Although I wish we were meeting under different circumstances, I am so glad we found each other. It makes me sad to know that the darkness that often comes with addiction has entered your life. I know that pain all too well. I am here to help you find that brightness, restore strength, and build hope for a better future for yourself.

There is a reason that if you squint your eyes and look at the front cover of this book, you will see **SAVING ME**. I created this book, podcasts, support group and community for individuals like you who know the turmoil that comes from loving an addict or losing someone to addiction and are ready to save themselves.

Using the scientific study of positive psychology and human flourishing and my learned experience, I am here to support you on your journey back to **you** and **your** power. My mission is to help lift those knocked down from loving someone with an addiction, to leverage the resiliency skills and strategies needed to regain footing, safeguard mental health, and enhance well-being.

Before I get into all the powerful tools, support and learning opportunities, I will briefly share my story and how I got here.

MY STORY

Who I thought was the love of my life. My happily ever after, and my soul mate, turned out not to be. We invested nine years in building a life together. Nine years! My kids and I adored this person. Together we took holidays, shared memories and enjoyed each other's company. He was funny, gentle, and full of life when we met. We had undeniable chemistry. He swept me off my feet and made me happy. We were excited about a future together. He was so loving and incredible with my kids. I thought to myself, how did I get so lucky? I loved him with all my heart. I believed in him more than anyone else and trusted him with all my heart. He was my person.

Intuitively and professionally, I knew something was off as time went on. The slow decline was concerning. I knew that he enjoyed alcohol, but I dismissed the problem. As his behaviour became more peculiar and his health declined, mentally and physically, I became suspicious. He started avoiding me when he once couldn't get enough of me. His temper became angrier and more hostile when he used to be gentle—followed by elation and playfulness. He became secretive and unapproachable. He would pick fights with me out of nowhere. I started to feel like I was hard to love, that maybe I was the problem. We, as a family, started walking on eggshells, trying to stay out of the line of fire. We even felt sorry for him, thinking perhaps he had chronic sinus infections, maybe depression or even had bipolar. Confused and concerned, we didn't know what was happening, but he was not himself. He was no longer the person we fell in love with anymore. Something was off, and I was determined to find out what it was. I became obsessed with trying to help him because I am a caring, kind-natured person. My professional training is in psychology, coaching, and resilience. After all, I should be able to help with the problem. Besides, that is what you do when you love someone. Right?

I became exhausted and stressed due to this strange behaviour, constant concern for his health, and worried about the future of our relationship.

Then I discovered the truth. I found out what was going on. I was tipped off and couldn't believe he had hidden this from me for so long. Finally, I had answers. An explanation for all the bizarre behaviour. Why the strange behaviour? Why the endless nights up in the garage? Why the paranoia? Why the picking of fights? Why the stealing of money? I was angry and felt stupid. He betrayed me and took advantage of me. But most of all, I was shocked. It was like the curtain opened, and I finally had answers to all my questions. Knowing about the addiction didn't make it easier. It became more challenging. Things got worse.

I often felt like loving an addict is like mourning the loss of someone still alive.

Active addiction began taking a firmer hold, and now I knew what was happening. Despite my apprehension and concern, we tried to make things work as my addicted loved one insisted he didn't have a problem, although his actions spoke otherwise. Although he denied the addiction, it started getting uglier and uglier. It amazes me how much I put up with it at that time. The manipulation, lies, betrayal, sleepless nights, and endless worry became the norm. I felt so concerned and kept offering loving support to try and help him. It was an ongoing quest. He completely broke me down and became a painful distraction.

I felt broken.

I would ask myself, "Why does he choose drugs over me?" Feeling heartbroken and confused by his choices. I lost myself trying to save, rescue, and help him. I was relentlessly fighting for the man I loved so dearly. I had lost my healthy values, boundaries and self-worth. My world revolved around him, his needs, and his struggles. As he became more and more important and the focus of my life, I was slowly getting lost. I was struggling. I would have done anything to help him get better. I only wished he would become the person I fell in love with again. I wanted so badly to find him amongst this new empty vessel of a human he had become. I got glimmers of hope, false promises, and small acts of love that would keep me around longer than I should have.

Trying to honour my needs and values, I set many boundaries, only to be broken. I felt stupid for putting up with all this turmoil and taking him back again and again. But ironically, I was acting like any person would when they love someone! After all, isn't the expression, until death do us part? Exhausted, depleted, angry, and drained, I realized I could not keep doing this; I couldn't live like this anymore. I often said to myself, Saving you is killing me! I got to the point where I realized no matter how hard I try, love, and care, I cannot control his addiction, I cannot cure his addiction, and I am not the cause of his addiction.

I was there, the lowest on the totem pole, languishing and struggling because of someone else's "problem." My world revolved around figuring out my loved one's addiction, trying to save him and grasping hard to get our lives back to normal. But, as his addiction worsened, he pulled me into his darkness. I was drowning myself. I lost my sparkle. I was distracted and worried constantly and put on a brave face trying to keep things together. Out of balance, alone, and feeling like I had lost myself and the love of my life, It became apparent something desperately needed to change. I had to start picking up the pieces of my broken heart and needed to restore wellness and save myself.

I found the courage to focus on myself.

And so I did! I literally scraped off all the black spray paint that my addicted loved one sprayed on the garage windows and started letting the sunlight back into my life. And you can too! The first step to taking back my life was the day I decided to put **myself** first.

And I am here to help you do the same!

And so, my journey began. I started focusing on picking up the pieces of my heart and focusing on my healing. I drew on my psychology and resilience training. I reached out for support. Sadly, I was not alone. I went on a mission to reclaim myself and my life. I put myself first and restored my happiness, peace and well-being.

Nothing prepares you for the pain and suffering of loving or losing someone to addiction. The pain and struggle I went through, and then the heartache when I discovered his addiction, would make him unrecognizable. I had lost the person I loved to addiction. He abandoned us, my two kids and me. He completely disappeared and discarded us like a used piece of chewing gum. The sadness was hard to endure. I can't even describe the sadness that I felt at that time. We were thrown away in what seemed as easy as tossing garbage in the trash.

I know my experience is not isolated, which makes me sad. Addiction is an animal that no one can go up against to fight. I have come a long way, and I promised myself I would not put my struggle to waste. I decided to write this book and build the SYKM community, where the struggle of loving someone with an addiction meets the science of human flourishing. I turned my pain into purpose. I advocate for supporting those battling similar battles, from loving or losing someone to addiction.

Now, I can honestly say his addiction and leaving were one of the best things that have ever happened to me. My healing journey has been full of ups and downs and has taken time. I want you to know from the bottom of my heart that you are worthy of love, joy, and happiness. I want you to know that you are worthy of being treated with respect, deserving of happiness, and are supposed to live joyfully in this life. Please don't let someone else's addiction damage the person you are meant to be for one second more.

Please remember you are not alone in this struggle. I am sending hugs, and I hope you enjoy the support offered in this book!

SAFEGUARD YOUR MENTAL HEALTH AND WELL-BEING

Saving You Is Killing Me: Loving Someone With an Addiction is a book devoted to **you**. That's the problem with putting addiction first: you've been coming in second! To be and give your best, you must start putting yourself first. Most of us are taught early on that being selfless is good, and kindness has many proven benefits. However, when you love (or have lost) someone to addiction, sometimes we can take the message to be giving of yourself to an extreme. Leaving us burned out, exhausted and feeling taken advantage of often.

When you love someone struggling with addiction (whether it's your partner, a family member or a friend), it's common to prioritize thinking about their well-being, needs, interests, challenges and so on. After all, you want to make those you love happy and feel heard and understood. But loving others doesn't mean that you can't love yourself too.

Prioritizing your well-being is essential to your well-being and up to you!

As you read the pages of this book, you will notice a common theme of self-compassion, self-care, courage and community. I call them the four c's of taking back your power. The thread throughout the book points to safeguarding your mental health and well-being, not prioritizing your addicted loved one or trying to manage their addiction. The focus of this book is to support **you** and build **your** resilience. Please put this learning into practice and do the supportive exercises and activities alongside each chapter. You can find additional activities, exercises and support in the *Saving You Is Killing Me: Loving Someone With an Addiction* Workbook.

We all sustain emotional wounds throughout life, and navigating someone else's addiction takes the challenge to a new level. Stress, guilt, rejection, and loss are as much a part of life as the occasional scraped elbow. And when you love someone with addiction, the wounds are not always visible. But while we typically bandage a cut or ice a sprained ankle, our first aid kit for emotional injuries is not just understocked; it's nonexistent at times. I was unprepared for the stresses, challenges, and abuse of addiction. No one really understands the incredible pain, stress and sadness that loving someone with an addiction can bring until they have been through it themselves.

You are not alone.

Healing from rejection, guilt, trauma, failure, and other everyday hurts requires resilience and prioritizing your mental health and well-being. *Saving You Is Killing Me: Loving Someone With an Addiction* is an essential book for anyone contemplating and ready to become more resilient, build self-esteem, and let go of the hurts and betrayals that could be holding you back.

When you catch yourself saying, "enough is enough," and you are ready to take back your power, this book is for you. Fortunately, there are measures you can take to build resilience and ways to safeguard your mental health and well-being to help you get unstuck, embrace change and take back your power. Drawing on the latest scientific research on human flourishing and using real-life examples, as a positive psychology expert, I offer you specific step-by-step proven strategies that are powerful and effective.

ABOUT THE EVIDENCE

This book is firmly grounded in research. When making a statement such as "Resilience helps facilitate well-being and promotes happiness," it can be supported by research results. For those who want to learn more, I invite you to my website www.savingyouiskillingme.com or refer to the end of this book, where there is a wealth of information about the research underlying well-being, resilience and happiness.

LET'S GET STARTED

Now, let's get started. I don't want you to waste any more time letting someone else's addiction damage the beautiful person you are meant to be and the extraordinary life you are meant to live.

Putting yourself first and prioritizing your well-being will help you safeguard your mental health so you can live joyfully. Learning and practicing the tools of resilience and human flourishing are steps to help you regain your power. The common four themes and resilience pillars throughout this book are:

SELF-COMPASSION: this encompasses being warm and understanding toward yourself when you suffer, fail or feel inadequate, rather than ignoring your pain or being self-critical.

SELF-CARE: is about taking good care of yourself and honouring your needs and values.

COURAGE: is trusting in your ability to bounce back from adversity and draw on your strengths and resources.

COMMUNITY: knowing you are not alone and permitting yourself to be human through struggle. Be sure to join our community. Here is the website to connect. www.savingyouiskillingme.com

CHAPTER ONE

It's Not Supposed to Be This Way: Reclaim Your Power and Build Resilience

Ships don't sink because of the water around them;
ships sink because of the water that gets in them.
Don't let what is happening around you
get inside you and weigh you down. — Adage

In this chapter, you will discover:

- The realities of addiction.
- Insights into what you Do have control over.
- What is recovery, and who benefits from recovery?
- What is resilience, and why is it essential to regain your well-being?
- What the science of well-being is, and how human flourishing can help you.
- What is the concept of struggling well?
- What self-advocacy is and why you must advocate for yourself.

Let's embark on a journey back to you, your joy, and your happiness while facing adversity so you can struggle well.

FACING THE ADVERSITY OF ADDICTION

Adversity is a regular part of life, and no person is immune to challenges. Addiction brings darkness, confusion, and turmoil, to a new level. It is incredibly taxing and beyond painful to love someone with, or have lost someone to, addiction. I bet you feel taken down, depleted, and broken and think quite literally, Saving You Is Killing Me. Loving someone with addiction was one of the biggest struggles I have ever endured. There comes a time when you need to decide to save yourself. Facing adversity head-on while building my resilience became my lifeline. Since you can't just bury your head in the sand and pretend things are okay, learning how to support yourself through this time of adversity becomes powerful.

Loving someone with an addiction is hard!

Sometimes, life is just hard. I can imagine you never anticipated being in a situation where you love someone with an addiction. No one ever really understands the adversity that comes with loving someone with addiction until they are in that situation themselves. Despite the sleepless nights, stress, and continual worry, I bet all too often, you wake up, face the world, and put on a brave face. I know I did. You might feel like you are going down the longest and most challenging road, and it might be getting to the point where being strong is the only option. But it's getting harder and harder to stay strong. You might even catch yourself lying to others that all is well.

I'm here to tell you that feeling broken, traumatized, and exhausted from loving someone with an addiction does not mean you are weak! I bet you are bearing the weight and burden of more than you care to admit while holding back the heartache of continued disappointment and stress. I know how you feel. You might feel uncertainty, anxiety, and loneliness that are breaking you down or have already broken you down.

I am here to tell you that this vulnerability is not a weakness! Taking back your power is not only about being strong and getting through this challenge - it is about becoming more resilient and compassionate while taking good care of yourself. Loving someone with an addiction can be traumatic. And I want you to know it's okay to admit this is one of the hardest things to navigate. It was for me too.

SAVING YOU IS KILLING ME: LOVING SOMEONE WITH AN ADDICTION

It is common to experience shame, anxiety, sleepless nights, and emotional pain that often stem from loving someone struggling with addiction. No matter what happens with your loved one, know that you can regain your power. You can prioritize your self-care and your healing. When addiction takes over a marriage or relationship, you may hardly recognize the person you once fell in love with. You may have lost yourself too. When addiction takes your child away, stress and worry can take over your life. Anyone married to, in a relationship with, or a parent of an addict knows that addiction is destructive. Addiction is damaging.

It's not supposed to be this way.

Just like the elephant in the room would be large and distracting, you can't wish it away, but you can say, "I see it. I am suffering. And I care about myself." If you are grieving or suffering, it is common to isolate yourself and push yourself through trying to be 'strong.' The bottom line is that it is devastating and damaging when you love someone with an addiction. My goal is that this book offers you an excellent source of loving support while you endure the pain that often comes when you love or have lost someone to addiction. You need to know that you are not alone and that there are many things you can do to build yourself back up. But let's first look at the realities of addiction.

REFLECTION QUESTIONS:

- What has been your biggest struggle?
- How has addiction affected you?
- What are your hopes to get out of this book?

THE REALITIES OF ADDICTION

It is common to misunderstand why or how other people become addicted. It is widely assumed to think that those with addiction may lack willpower or moral decision-making and could stop simply by choosing to stop. In reality, addiction is a very complex and, some would say, disease. According to the National Institute on Drug Abuse, Addiction changes the brain in ways that make quitting hard, even for those who want to. From the science, research, and professionals in their fields, the consensus is that some realities of addiction might offer you a degree of support.

When you are armed with these realities, advocating for yourself, healing, and regaining your power becomes possible. Many psychologists, counsellors and recovery groups suggest variations of the following truths of addiction:

You did not cause the addiction: You are not at fault. As a parent or a significant other of someone addicted, it is widespread to think that you have done something to cause the addiction. Not to mention, people addicted are very likely to blame others for their use. Still, it is merely an attempt to justify the addict's actions. It is essential to recognize that it's not about you. Knowing that you are not the cause of the addiction lifts any guilt, shame and blame that often is associated with addiction.

Truth: Nothing you do causes addiction in another person.

No one expects to become an addict: Although addictions start with a choice, many people who try a drug, for example, will not get hooked. There's no easy way to understand what causes one person to become addicted compared to another. It's essential to recognize that no one expects to become an addict. This awareness can compassionately help with understanding addiction.

Truth: No one expects addiction to take hold.

You cannot control their addiction: You can't control an addict's behaviour. No matter how much you try to control another's behaviour, regardless of addiction, you do not have control over any other human. Many consider addiction a disease that starts with a choice and heavily affects brain chemistry. You are not able to control your loved one who is struggling with addiction. Addiction is more powerful than you.

Truth: You have no control over another human's addiction.

You cannot cure their addiction: Unfortunately, there is no simple cure for addiction. You can do nothing to save or fix the addicted person. They have to want to seek help. They have to choose recovery. You cannot do this for another human. As much as you want and desire to help your loved one get better, nothing you do will help cure their addiction.

Truth: You cannot cure your loved one's addiction.

You are powerless over their addiction: Powerlessness is often mistaken for weakness, but this is a vital realization. As a caring human, you might believe you need to take control, be proactive, fix problems, and help others, especially when they are struggling. Admitting powerlessness involves leaning into surrendering the things you can't control. Addiction makes no exception. You may be powerless over an addiction but not over your mental health and prioritizing your well-being. I've never liked the expression: you are powerless; it sounds hopeless. Remember, you might be powerless when it comes to someone else's addiction, but you are influential in your own life and well-being. The sad truth is that there isn't much you can do for your addicted loved one. The great truth is you can save yourself, prioritize your well-being, and safeguard your mental health.

Truth: You are powerless over their addiction but powerful over yourself.

Knowing the realities of addiction helps you see what you can't do and have no control over. This book is about regaining your power and building resilience so you can live life happier. Now, let's look at what you do have control over and what you **can** do.

REFLECTION QUESTIONS:

- What has been the most challenging reality of addiction?
- Why?

WHAT YOU DO HAVE CONTROL OVER, AND WHAT YOU CAN DO

Do you feel like no matter what you are doing isn't working? If you love someone with an addiction, you no doubt feel overwhelmed and desperate to offer help, wishing they will come to their senses. It is expected for you to question why the addict loves their addiction more than they love you, and consequently, you are hoping the addict will see how much addiction is destroying their life.

It becomes essential to save yourself. It's hard to love an addicted person and stay healthy. The idea that you cannot control, change, or "fix" another person is disheartening. Still, you often keep trying while losing yourself in the process. You might notice no matter what you try, it isn't working. I was there too. Going up against addiction is challenging and often a no-win situation or losing battle.

I remember thinking: "If only you could love someone hard enough to make them stop doing drugs." It is common to think: "They do not love me enough to stop." Addiction brings unrelenting heartache. The struggle that comes with loving someone with an addiction can be very damaging for those around it. That is why they say addiction is a family disease. It often leaves bystanders feeling helpless and in the line of fire.

Although this book is written non-denominational, there is great value in The *Serenity Prayer*. Please take or leave any part that resonates with you.

> *God grant me the serenity to accept*
> *the things I cannot change,*
> *the courage to change the things I can,*
> *and the wisdom to know the difference.*

The *Serenity Prayer* means letting go of situations beyond your control and taking action toward things within your control. In other words, letting go of trying to control addiction, focusing on yourself and your well-being, and safeguarding your mental health.

When armed with the realities of addiction and the message of the *Serenity Prayer*, you can start to advocate for yourself. Please don't wait for your situation to get worse or for your addicted loved one to seek recovery. Choose yourself now. Regain your power. You are worthy of self-care, self-love, and self-compassion.

REFLECTION QUESTIONS:

- How do the realities of addiction help you?
- What does the *Serenity Prayer* mean to you?
- How do the realities of addiction and the words of the *Serenity Prayer* help you take back your power?

TAKING CARE OF YOURSELF IS NOT GIVING UP ON THEM.

Taking care of yourself is not giving up on them. It simply means you love yourself enough to take good care of yourself. I distinctly remember the turning point; I had an anxiety attack and a mental breakdown. I can't express the hurt in my heart, the anger in my fists, and the confusion in my mind. I remember feeling broken. I had to surrender to the realities of addiction. I had to **save myself**. I had to stop fighting for the relationship we once had, the person he used to be, and make my life about healing and regaining my sparkle. I am here to help you do the same.

I know that it is so painful not being able to help when the person you love is destroying themselves. To watch someone you love go down such a dark path and become an empty vessel of a human is devastating. But you cannot allow them to pull you into their muck or quicksand. You will both struggle if you get pulled onto the roller coaster. You were not born to suffer. You deserve peace, joy, and a sense of safety. It is not supposed to be this way.

That's the problem with putting addiction first: you've been coming in second! Self-care is critical when you feel empty and have nothing left to give. When enough is enough, and you are ready to put yourself first, or at least attempt to prioritize yourself, your healing will begin. You deserve a break. Self-care is not selfish. It is necessary! You make less space for the addiction when you fill up with self-care. It does not mean you are giving up on your addicted loved one. It means you are also not giving up on yourself. Caring for yourself never takes away from others. It is essential to learn to create inner calm and peace within yourself instead of focusing on others.

Some of the best self-care practices to incorporate to help you take care of your well-being are essential and often overlooked: journaling, Coaching or Therapy, Exercise, Meditation, Healthy/Nutritious Eating, Adequate Sleep, Healthy Boundaries, Solitude/Unplugging, and Stress Management. Pick some of these and add them to your self-care routine right away. Self-care is crucial to the recovery process. There are many more ways to support you throughout this book to help you regain your power, find joy in your life, and transform your well-being. It is about building the case to prioritize your well-being and advocate for yourself.

REFLECTION QUESTIONS:

- What does it mean to you to take care of yourself?
- Why is it essential to prioritize your well-being now?

RECOVERY: NOT JUST FOR THE ADDICT

Have you been told the following?

- You are addicted to the addict.
- You are co-dependent.
- You have a problem.
- You're an enabler.
- Work the program.
- You need recovery.

I know this is common. You get told these things that point to blame and shame and make a challenging situation even more damaging. You might be thinking, Why do I need recovery? What do I need to be in recovery for? I am not an addict. I want you to see recovery from a new perspective, one that is full of self-compassion and support.

What does it mean to be in addiction recovery?

It means you are working on successfully managing your addiction and regaining control of your life. Once you recover from your addiction, you are in recovery for the rest of your life. Recovery involves healing mentally, physically, and emotionally from your addiction abuse and the causes of your addiction.

Recovery is commonly associated with the person who is addicted. But the truth is: We need recovery too. Typical addict behaviour in relationships involves neglecting all their relationships and only spending time with the people who share their addiction. Their sleeping and eating habits will change dramatically, and they will often blame it on something else. Addiction can seriously damage relationships, from distrust and abusive behaviour to health complications and mental illness. Think about the typical behaviour of an addict.

- Addicts are irresponsible
- Addicts may be depressed
- Addicts can be abusive
- Addicts rely on deception

- Addicts manipulate
- Addicts will become distant
- Addicts' behaviours change
- Addicts often disappear unexpectedly.
- Addicts often steal.
- Addicts often lie.
- Addicts can't be trusted.
- Addicts are not reliable.
- Addicts' behaviour is unpredictable.

How addicts behave in relationships can pose a real struggle for a partner, parent or friend. It is no wonder recovery is necessary. You need to recover from the addict in your life!

But let's look at the definition again.

Recovery is about hope, healing, and health.

I offer you a no-shame or blame finger-pointing perspective on recovery. Recovery is about changing your life to recover or to get you back. When you leave a wallet at the store and return to get it, you recover it. Are you ready to reclaim yourself? Get you back? It's easy to get lost in the muck of addiction. Recovery is essential, but let's look at it from the perspective of compassion and empowerment.

New Definition of Recovery:

- Recovery is a process of change through which people improve their health and wellness, live self-directed lives, and strive to reach their full potential.
- Recovery is for everyone- not just the addict. This type of recovery is not admitting fault, blame or shame around your influence on the addict. It recognizes you want to regain your power and prioritize your well-being. A tiny shift in perspective can help you tremendously!
- Recovery is any process during which a person attempts to overcome a challenge affecting their health, wellness, and daily life.

Loving someone with an addiction is hard. And no one knows this struggle unless they have gone through it themselves. The promise of recovery offers hope. Hope is believing in a better future for yourself, attached to no one else's behaviour. Recovery means different things to different people. Recovery can be a joyful journey of healing and transformation, enabling you to live a meaningful life while striving to achieve your full potential.

So next time someone tells you to "Work the program," "You need recovery." or "You are addicted to the addict." Pause and think: There is nothing wrong with me, but I may have been affected or damaged by someone else's addiction that has broken me down. It's time to seek recovery and healing. Picking up this book is a powerful step in your recovery journey.

Pillars of Recovery:

Three pillars of recovery include self-awareness, self-acceptance, and integration/application. These simple rules can help you understand that recovery is not complicated or beyond your control. To recover, it involves these characteristics:

1. Change your life.
2. Be completely honest with yourself.
3. Ask for help.
4. Practice self-care.
5. Don't bend the rules and prioritize your well-being.

REFLECTION QUESTIONS:

- How will you improve your health?
- How will you improve your well-being?
- Who are you at your best?
- What is your full potential?
- Where are you now? Honestly?
- Where do you want to make changes?
- Who can you reach out to for support?
- What can you do to get help?
- What daily habits can you implement?

RESILIENCE: AN ESSENTIAL INGREDIENT TO SAFE-GUARD WELL-BEING

Putting yourself first is essential to building resilience, regaining power and safeguarding your mental health. But what exactly is resilience, and why is it necessary for our happiness? Let's discuss resilience, human flourishing and positive psychology.

Resilience is coping with a mental and emotional crisis and a return to well-being. You can bounce back from adversity. Resilience is something you can grow and use to enhance your well-being. This entire book is devoted to building your resilience. It is not a 'happiology' or pretend positivity, but rather the development of your ability to protect yourself from stressors' potential adverse effects. Resilience helps you return to a baseline of well-being.

According to one of the most influential authors of psychology textbooks and social psychologists, Dr. David G. Myers, well-being is a healthy, comfortable, and happy state. Research suggests that certain intentional behaviours can help improve your well-being by creating positive feelings and a sense of reward and giving you feelings of self-worth and purpose as they help you connect with others.

Resilience is about bouncing back after difficult times and your capacity to deal with challenges while still holding your head up. Resilience is about being able to cope with whatever life throws at you. It is also about adapting well to adversity, trauma, tragedy, and threats. Building resilience is essential when you love someone with an addiction.

Building resilience and prioritizing your well-being enables you to develop protection and support mechanisms when you feel overwhelmed. It will help you maintain balance during difficult and stressful periods. Resilience can protect you from anxiety, depression, and mental health difficulties. You are designed to bounce back, and life is not supposed to be a constant struggle. Resilience is the key to regaining your power. Although this book is devoted to building resilience, you can build resilience by

- Finding purpose, making contributions or being of service.
- Believing in yourself, your abilities and your strengths.
- Developing a social network, connections and building relationships.
- Embracing change and healthy perspective with competence and confidence.
- Being optimistic, creating a positive outlook, and practicing hopefulness.
- Nurturing and caring for yourself.

- Developing problem-solving skills and coping strategies.
- Establishing goals, taking action and building skills over time.

How you cope and adapt to tragic events or stressful situations is vital for your well-being. Being resilient will help you move from being stuck to being able to move forward. Everybody has resilience. Being resilient doesn't mean you don't feel the intensities that come from loving someone with an addiction. It means you have found good ways of dealing with the challenge quicker and more effectively. It is about your ability to struggle well.

Psychological resilience is coping mentally and emotionally to overcome setbacks, adversity, crisis, or trauma. Resilience training applies positive psychological interventions and tools to strengthen your mental fitness and bounce-back thinking. The great news is that everybody can learn to increase their ability to be more resilient.

REFLECTION QUESTIONS:

- What does resilience mean to you?
- When and how have you been resilient in the past?
- How can you start building resilience today?

THE SCIENCE BEHIND WELL-BEING AND HUMAN FLOURISHING

Human flourishing is the ability to live a good life. It is the optimal continuing development of human potential and living well as a human being. It is about being engaged in relationships and activities that are meaningful and joyful. It doesn't mean you are happy all the time. *Flourish*ing is when people experience positive emotions, positive psychological functioning and positive social functioning, most of the time. Resilience in positive psychology describes our ability to cope with life's challenges. It encourages you to focus on the right things to build resilience and foster human flourishing.

*Flourish*ing is when you feel connected and purposeful; the opposite of flourishing is languishing or feeling lacklustre or disconnected. Languishing is a sense of stagnation and emptiness. It feels as if you're muddling through your days, looking at your life through foggy glasses. Corey Keyes, an American sociologist and psychologist, known for his work with positive psychology, described languishing as emptiness and stagnation, constituting a life of quiet despair. It is characterized by dissatisfaction, lack of engagement, and apathy. I was languishing when I was in the muck of someone else's addiction, and you most likely are as well and maybe not aware of it.

A thorough understanding of the conditions that enable human flourishing will promote safety and security. Well-being is fundamental to your health and overall happiness. Having a strong and well-adapted sense of well-being can help you overcome adversity. Feelings of well-being are fundamental to an individual's overall health, enabling them to overcome difficulties and achieve their desires.

Each person is a unique individual with different goals and desires. However, there is one hope we all share: to live a good life. One of the first steps is realizing life isn't supposed to be a struggle, filled with stress and chaos all the time. As a human, you are meant to flourish and thrive. Yes, there will be ups and downs, but you can still flourish and be happy. It is common to be dispirited or discouraged when you love someone with an addiction. Positive psychology is a field of study devoted to helping you be resilient, flourish and struggle well.

"Positive Psychology is about what makes life worth living."
— Dr. Christopher Peterson

What is Positive Psychology?
Positive Psychology is the scientific study of what leads to happiness, well-being, and flourishing lives. It results from being aware of self-development opportunities and

the courage to take advantage of them. The key here is to recognize that it takes courage to prioritize your version of the good life. Resilience and human flourishing are available to you. They are skills you can get better at through practice and application. You can build up your reserve of resilience. Resilience gives you a sense of agency- the feeling that you can improve and influence your life.

As a field, positive psychology encompasses thinking about topics like character strengths, optimism, life satisfaction, happiness, well-being, gratitude, compassion (as well as self-compassion), self-esteem and self-confidence, hope, and elevation.

You have the power to influence your life and regain your strength.

Have I convinced you to choose yourself and prioritize your well-being yet? One of the first steps is deciding you deserve and need to come first. Then it's about applying intentional behaviours to support your well-being. I am not suggesting to pretend the challenge of loving someone with an addiction isn't going on around you, but rather, to advocate for your well-being during this struggle.

The science behind well-being and human flourishing are available to everyone.

At an introductory level, you can develop your abilities to flourish by

1. Being committed to growing and learning.
2. Developing, supportive and cultivating environments that build your capabilities.
3. Believing in yourself and your abilities.
4. Knowing about your health and how to be healthy.
5. Being self-motivated to achieve goals that you value.
6. Setting up strong support systems and connections with others.

REFLECTION QUESTIONS:

- What would the good life look like for you?
- Knowing we all can flourish, how will you prioritize your well-being?

STRUGGLE WELL: A POSITIVE PSYCHOLOGY APPROACH TO CHALLENGE

We all want fulfillment, connection, and purpose, as well as to progress in life. Humans also desire growth, love, and peace. To struggle well, we must understand that everyone struggles. It is universal to experience challenges, a part of life that cannot be avoided. It makes sense that you struggle when you love someone with an addiction. What is important here is to struggle well, embracing the inevitable struggle.

Two Approaches to Struggle:

- The conventional ways of dealing with trauma often leave people feeling stuck, damaged, and as though they have been sentenced to life as a diminished version of themselves, and
- The struggle-well path encourages the opportunity to use trauma and struggle to create more significant meaning, deeper purpose, and a more authentic and fulfilling life.

Experiencing struggle is inevitable and applicable to your growth and learning, allowing you to tap into and build resilience. It also makes you look deep inside yourself to find the answers and strength. When you accept struggle as part of the human experience, you stop giving others control and start looking inside yourself for support. When you look inside, you begin to see what's right, what you can do and what resonates deep within you. Struggling well allows you to claim a new perspective, build resilience and flourish. This perspective proclaims that you have been through or are going through difficult times and don't want to survive merely; you want to thrive.

REFLECTION QUESTIONS:

- How are you struggling the best you can right now?
- Where do you feel stuck?
- What are you most proud of during this challenge?
- How does the struggle-well mindset help you?

ADVOCATE FOR YOURSELF

Taking care of yourself means realizing that you're also important. It means not ignoring your needs and the things that make you feel good. It can be best described as helping others by helping yourself first. It means prioritizing your happiness and fulfillment without infringing on others. Engaging in self-care, self-love, and self-compassion is proven to reduce or eliminate anxiety and depression, reduce stress, improve concentration, minimize frustration and anger, increase happiness, improve energy, and more.

I am sure you have heard the expression to put your oxygen mask on first. That is because putting your oxygen mask on means taking care of yourself. When you fly on an airplane, the flight attendant instructs you to "put your oxygen mask on first" before helping others. For parents, this may seem rather unbelievable! But, if you don't take care of yourself, you are useless to those who need your support.

Another similar message is to say, "You can't pour from an empty cup"? Essentially, the proverb means that for humans to take care of others effectively, we must first take care of ourselves. The notion is intuitive but can be more challenging to put into practice. Further to this idea, it would be best if you poured from your overflow, not your reserve, to stay strong and resilient. In other words, fill up your cup with an overflow of abundance and only give away what is extra. Never depleting your won reserves. It all starts with you and prioritizing your well-being.

Save yourself. Everyone is on different paths and at various stages. Still, sometimes you need a little support and reminders of your resilience. You have resilience in you! I am wrapping you in love and wish we had met under different circumstances. I was there, the lowest on the totem pole, languishing and struggling because of someone else's "problem."

If you feel like you are drowning, you can give up and struggle or push against the bottom and come up for air, but it's up to you!

Self-advocacy means you know your rights and what you deserve.

You know what is fair, speak up for your rights, and make choices and decisions that take care of you. Self-advocacy is a skill you need when you love someone with an addiction.

Starting now, it's all about you. Not your addicted loved one. You can build your resiliency and shift your focus to advocating for yourself. Are you ready to become more resilient and struggle well, even when you care about someone with an addiction? It is time to start caring for yourself. If you are ready and convinced, you need to find the courage to focus on yourself to help regain your power. Finish the declaration statement below.

Declaration statement:

I _____ am worthy of prioritizing my well-being and am choosing to safeguard my mental health. I no longer come second to addiction. I choose me first. I am excited to focus on myself and put my life back together. I deserve peace and happiness.

KEY TAKE-AWAYS

- ✓ Adversity is a part of life, and loving someone with addiction makes no exception. Addiction is terrible.

- ✓ Focusing on yourself will help you regain power, build resilience, and safeguard your mental health.

- ✓ Recovery is about hope, healing, and health. Recovery is about changing your life to recover or to get you back.

- ✓ Resilience is a skill you can learn, grow and cultivate through practice and application.

- ✓ Challenge is an inevitable part of life, and it is possible to struggle well through life's ups and downs.

- ✓ Healing starts with you and your courage to advocate for your well-being.

CHAPTER REFLECTION QUESTIONS:

Take a moment to write down your highlights from this chapter:

- What takeaways are going to inspire you the most going forward?

_____

_____

_____

_____

_____

_____

- What brought a significant or slight shift in your thinking, feelings, or behaviour?

_____

_____

_____

_____

_____

_____

CHAPTER TWO

It's Okay Not to Be Okay: Build Self-Awareness and Give Yourself the Permission to Be Human

"What we don't need in the midst of struggle is shame for being human." — *Brene Brown*

FROM POWERLESS TO POWERFUL USING SELF-AWARENESS

You may often feel fragile and broken, but you are strong and resilient. To feel hurt is to be human. Are you gazing at the clock, waiting, worrying, wondering: When are they coming home? Are they okay? Where are they? What are they doing? What if _____ happens? You might be dealing with strange behaviours like hiding in the garage, leaving in the middle of the night, staying up all night, not coming home, and making a four-hour trip to the gas station, followed by sleeping for days. You might be seeing angry fits, mood swings, never knowing what version of a human you will get. You might catch them in lies, only to be manipulated, blamed, stolen from, and abandoned for days.

Anger, sadness, disappointment, confusion, contempt, disbelief, overwhelm, disgust, fear, and worry are just a few emotions that you might be experiencing. So many potential emotions come up when you love someone with an addiction, and rightfully so!! It's like being on a rollercoaster that you can't get off of without trauma and anguish. It becomes imperative that you support yourself.

"You can hurt me, but you can't break me down."
— *Rakesh Sahoo*

Self-awareness is about taking an honest look at your life without any attachment to it being right or wrong, good or bad. Self-awareness allows you to honour and understand what is happening inside your mind, thoughts, emotions, and beliefs. Your feelings are continually communicating with you. When you feel certain emotions, such as anger, it is a message that something is wrong in your environment, or you might perceive deception.

The great news is that you have control over thoughts and, therefore, emotions as well. As much as we humans want to control the circumstances around us, we are not in control of the events presented to us. That sounds scary, but another good news is we have influence!

Gaining self-awareness gives you the superpower you need to help navigate yourself through challenging situations and empowers you. Self-awareness gives you the power to change your thinking, change your emotions, influence where you focus your attention, control your feelings, and respond. Having self-awareness brings freedom, as it allows you to take control of your emotions and make the changes you desire. (The changes that you have influence over.)

When you love someone with an addiction, all too often, you are in a place of worry, stress, frustration, and fear. Negative emotions can begin to consume your mind and take over your life. It becomes expected that negative emotions burden your mind. To regain your power, you can deepen your self-awareness, understand your feelings, and monitor your thinking to step back into your power and influence. Let's face it; it's common to feel completely out of control when you love someone with an addiction. No matter what you do, nothing seems to help.

It is exciting to shift your energy back onto yourself by gaining self-awareness and influence.

In this book section, you will see yourself from the inside out. It will be about self-exploration without any judgment. It is common to numb feelings, hide pain, and struggle with worry and rumination. Self-awareness harnesses the power to tap into your mind and constructively honour your emotions, thoughts, and beliefs. What you continually think about becomes your world. The mind is one of the most substantial, valuable powers you possess. Regardless of what is going on and how powerless you feel, you influence your thoughts. Think about self-awareness like you're gaining self-knowledge through emotional exploration and self-management. Let's begin using self-awareness as a powerful tool to regain your power.

In this chapter, you will learn the following:
- What is self-awareness?
- Why it is essential to regain your power.
- How to use self-awareness for healing and empowerment.
- Specific tools to increase self-awareness.

WHAT IS SELF-AWARENESS?

When you love someone with addiction, emotions can get the better of you. Frequently you are left feeling hurt, disappointed, angry and sad. But it is essential to know these emotions are fundamental to your well-being and human. When you gain self-awareness, you can recognize and manage your feelings and gain emotional intelligence to help you regain your power and better handle these elements of your life. It is empowering to look at your own words and actions from a perspective outside of yourself to see yourself more clearly. In this sense, self-awareness is a way of introspection that brings opportunities for honouring your thoughts, feelings and behaviour from a straightforward, compassionate perspective.

Self-awareness is about seeing yourself through objectivity, reflection, introspection, and looking at yourself from the inside out. In positive psychology, it is called meta-cognition, where you think about your thinking. In other words, self-awareness is about perceiving your strengths, weaknesses, thoughts, beliefs, and emotions. As you develop more self-awareness, you can change the thoughts and interpretations that you might have made in your mind.

Sometimes your mind will go to autopilot, where it might run off worrying, ruminating, or even storytelling. The mind is incredible and geared toward keeping you safe. It can even get hijacked into a stress response or a panic attack simply from our thinking and interpretations. This awareness and understanding of how our thoughts, perceptions, interpretations, and beliefs influence our emotions and affect our actions can become exceptionally empowering.

Self-awareness involves monitoring your feelings, your thoughts, and your beliefs. It becomes a tool to help you reach higher levels of well-being and overall happiness. It can even bring a sense of calm in the chaos. When you create space between the stimulus (or what hooks you in), the stressor or circumstance, and your reaction to it, you generate room to look in between and gain an empowering perspective. In other words, self-awareness gives us space to respond instead of reacting, which feels empowering.

Self-awareness can be cultivated and practised. It's like a muscle; the more you practice, the stronger you get. Each moment is an opportunity to be self-aware.

We commonly suppress, hide, or disregard our feelings. Sometimes we even suffer in silence. When you love someone with an addiction, there can be shame and embarrassment. It is typical to numb, hide and struggle on your own. Emotions need our attention. If emotions are ignored, they will get louder. Self-awareness is the key to intentionally honouring and successfully processing your feelings that come up. Observing and honouring your thoughts, feelings, and beliefs is essential.

Simply put, self-awareness refers to an awareness of yourself on many different levels: whether that be your emotions, your preferences, your intentions, your values, or your beliefs. Emotional intelligence is the ability to use, understand, and positively manage your emotions to relieve stress and overcome challenges. When you are more self-aware, you gain intelligence over your feelings. You can gain a perspective that feels better. You start to honour your truth and see things through a compassionate lens. With self-awareness, you can shift from a place of helplessness to responsibility.

REFLECTION QUESTIONS:

- What circumstances have triggered emotions inside you?
- What emotions are you feeling right now?
- Where do you feel it in your body?
- What thought did you have that led to those emotions?

As these feelings come up, observe them for what they are. State the emotion you are feeling. Give yourself love around those feelings. It's okay not to be okay. Negative emotions like sadness, anger, loneliness, frustration, self-criticism, fear, or rejection can sometimes be tricky, even painful. The concept of self-awareness is about knowing emotions are human, that you are human. It's okay not to be okay. When we love someone with an addiction, it's brutal, sad and devastating to watch someone you love destroy themselves. Your feelings are natural and human.

WHAT IS EMOTIONAL AGILITY?

Do emotions like fear and anger drive you, or do you try to avoid these feelings altogether? You likely need to learn to become emotionally agile while navigating the challenges of loving someone with an addiction. Self-awareness allows us to be emotionally agile. According to the Google dictionary, emotional intelligence is the capacity to be aware of, control, and express one's emotions and handle interpersonal relationships judiciously and empathetically. Agility is about the ability to move, understand and adapt quickly.

All the emotions you feel, good or bad, are signals that will help you navigate through life. It makes sense that you are experiencing these emotions because you are human. There is no shame or weakness in having certain feelings. Emotional agility will help you learn how to gain perspective on your emotional responses and discover a new way to move forward and make decisions that better serve you.

It is human to face unexpected detours, challenges, and setbacks. When you love someone with an addiction, the uncontrollable situation, turmoil, and uncertainty generate a very unsettling feeling. Emotional agility can help you manage these challenges or events that cause you to derail.

Do you experience self-doubt, shame, sadness, fear, or anger that sometimes too easily steer you in a hopeless direction? You are not immune to stresses and setbacks, especially when you love someone with an addiction. Susan David's book, Emotional Agility shows us how anyone can thrive in uncertainty by becoming more emotionally agile, whoever you are, and whatever you face. She talks about how, as humans, we are all prone to standard hooks that cause emotions such as self-doubt, shame, sadness, fear, or anger that can too quickly steer us in a hopeless direction.

Emotional agility or emotional intelligence is about loosening the grip of challenge, calming yourself down, and living with more intention. It's about choosing how you'll respond to your emotional warning system.

Author Susan David teaches us that there is space and opportunity between stimulus and response. The critical benefit of self-awareness is knowing how to adapt, aligning actions with values, and making small but powerful changes that lead to a lifetime of growth and happiness. Emotions and the ability to regulate them are what make you uniquely human. All emotions serve a function.

To gain more awareness, consider how evolutionary roles play a part in our emotions. For thousands of years, our brains have evolved. Our brain consists of two parts: the emotional brain (or lizard brain) and the rational brain (or neo-cortex). The lizard, or reptilian, is essential for survival, and our logical brain is the part that helps us ration or reason. They fight like the lizard brain going against the modern man. The lizard part of the brain is there to keep us safe and protect us. Sometimes when the lizard (emotional) part of the brain is pumping, it takes over the brain's rational part. Negative emotions serve an evolutionary role: protection and survival. As humans, we need to have feelings like worry, anger, and guilt to keep us safe. Negative emotions serve a role and function. The key is to avoid getting stuck in the emotional part of your brain.

It becomes crucial to learn to work with both parts of our brains. Self-awareness is an excellent tool to generate the compassion, understanding, and space you need to take care of yourself effectively. Emotional agility is not about ignoring difficult emotions and thoughts; it's about holding them loosely, facing them courageously and compassionately, and then moving past them to bring more peace, strength, and your best self forward.

Regardless of the turmoil that is going on around you, you must accept emotions as signals that can help you navigate life. There are reasons that you are experiencing these feelings! Humans can feel fear, sadness, guilt, contempt, disappointment, anger, etc. Why do negative emotions exist? Negative emotions are not a problem - rejecting their existence and considering them unfavourable is the problem. I know firsthand how preoccupied your world becomes when you love someone with an addiction. Your mind becomes hijacked by worry, concern, and heartache. But there is an important message here: no one can make you miserable unless you allow them to do so. Their problem is not your problem.

The bottom line is that you must feel your feelings and become agile to safeguard your mental health. Be present and feel emotions, step back, create distance, and take action based on your values and what is important to you. Let go, accept your decision, and move on. That is where your power lies. Let go of numbness and powerlessness by harnessing self-awareness and emotional agility.

REFLECTION QUESTIONS:

- What emotions need your attention right now?
- When you get present in the moment, what are you feeling?
- What do you value?
- What is important to you?
- What happens when you give your emotions space?

WHY SELF-AWARENESS IS IMPORTANT FOR REGAINING YOUR POWER

It's tiring acting okay when you're close to the edge of a breakdown and not okay. Many benefits come with self-awareness. When you focus on yourself rather than your environment or the people around you, you connect with your values, beliefs, and emotions. Emotions, whether negative or positive, have value and purpose. Controlling your emotions can be challenging. However, these emotions are communicating something to you. Self-awareness is the ability to step back and recognize the feelings that you are having. When you have an emotional response, it is like a flashing light or alarm bell trying to tell you something or get your attention.

Being aware of your emotions allows you to consciously choose how you might respond or whether you will respond at all. Self-awareness opens you up to different possibilities for behaviour. When you become more self-aware, you are better able to be an observer and a learner without judgment. According to the book Mindset and the research of Dr. Carol Dweck, mindset impacts resilience. When you hold a growth mindset that is curious and open to learning and growth, you are equipped to bounce back better than before.

A growth mindset is about shifting from being problem-focused to solution-focused. A fixed mindset tends to put you into a place of judgment and criticism while keeping you problem-focused. A growth mindset puts you into a place of learning and keeps you solution-focused. To get yourself into a place of resilience, you must learn to progress from a fixed mindset into a growth mindset. Resilience and bouncing back are all about what you do when you hit a bump in the road. When you hold a fixed mindset, you're more likely to say: "I am a failure," and show judgment towards the situation you face as if it is wrong or will never change. If you have a growth mindset, you won't judge yourself as having been a failure if something terrible happens.

Self-awareness is the key to noticing what mindset you might be operating with daily. A growth mindset helps bring about more grit, and grit enables you to persevere over obstacles and stay curious and hopeful.

Self-awareness helps you get unstuck from self-defeating stories, inner critic voices, and worries that might be out of your control. It operates like a powerful tool for regaining your power. The ups and downs of life that come with loving someone with an addiction create trauma, stress, and fear. It is easy to start and collect self-defeating stories, worrisome thoughts, and anger that get replayed.

I remember, to sleep, I would have to talk to myself and say: "Don't worry, Andrea, he is probably coming home in the morning like always and will be apologizing and begging for your forgiveness - it makes sense you are worried and frustrated, this is strange, disrespectful behaviour, but just go to sleep." Otherwise, my anger, worry, and resentment of him not coming home, not messaging me, or telephoning and my curiosity about where he was would keep me up all night. I had to regain control of my thinking and calm myself down to find peace and sleep.

Self-awareness can be a tool to bring you some peace and calm. How you navigate your inner world, thoughts, feelings, and self-talk ultimately determine how you experience life. You will have many stressors or catalysts that will push buttons and be triggers for you. The trauma, manipulation, and abuse that come with loving someone with an addiction is a massive test for your emotions. It is easy to feel hopeless and defeated and think the cycle will never end.

Self-awareness, a growth mindset, and emotional agility become essential to your balance. Stepping back and detaching from the chaos that comes with addiction allows you to embrace your core values, create boundaries, and adjust your actions in life. The following section offers actionable suggestions to help you gain self-awareness and regain your power through self-awareness.

CULTIVATE MINDFULNESS TO GAIN SELF-AWARENESS

Mindfulness is an ancient practice that moves you from mindlessness and run-away thoughts of worry, concern and rumination to mindfulness and the gain of the distance between the thinking and the thought. Pulling back from the runaway thinking to keep space can be powerful. Interestingly, Mindfulness is not just meditation; it isn't about wiping your mind clear of thoughts. It's not just relaxation; although calming, it's not a pose in yoga. According to the Greater Good Science Center at Berkeley, Mindfulness is: "maintaining a moment-by-moment awareness of our thoughts, feelings, bodily sensations, and the surrounding environment through a gentle, nurturing lens."

Many people go about their days mindlessly. Or the mind is taken over by worry. You might be asking questions like, Why are they acting this way? Where are they? Are they drinking/doing drugs again? Are they okay?

Why do they pick fights with me? What else can I do to help them? What if my boundaries are too rigid and something terrible happens? Your brain gets hijacked by thoughts like these.

Mindfulness and present-moment thinking are primary tools and antidotes to run-away thinking that doesn't make you feel good. Since your emotional brain can get hijacked, mindfulness is a beautiful tool to calm yourself down to a point where the rational brain can perform.

Mindfulness requires a nonjudgmental acknowledgment and acceptance of thoughts and feelings. Being mindful can pause the brain, bring yourself back to the present moment, and allow you to step back from your emotion and view them compassionately and curiously.

One of the world's foremost experts on mindfulness, Jon Kabat-Zinn, has summarized the experience of Mindfulness as "paying attention in a particular way; on purpose, in the present moment, and non-judgmentally." Moving from mindlessness to mindfulness can help you become more self-aware. From autopilot to being in the driver's seat. Through Mindfulness, you can become more immersed in the moment you are presently in and break out of the space of stress or worry.

According to Netta Weinstein's research in the Journal of Research in Personality, when stressors hit (as they do for all of us), individuals who regularly utilize mindfulness have been shown to engage in healthier and more effective coping strategies than their less mindful peers. Mindfulness enhances problem-solving, enabling us to make better choices.

HOW TO CULTIVATE MINDFULNESS

You can become mindful by connecting to your senses: Take time to reconnect to the present and gain distance from your inner chatterbox or worry box. You could say STOP, then connect to all your senses: What am I seeing? What am I smelling? What am I hearing? What am I feeling? Keep going and practice keeping your mind in the present moment. Take note of what you are sensing at any given moment; the sights, sounds, and smells typically go unnoticed. Another tool to be more mindful is to scan your body to mentally observe any areas of tension, stress, or strain so you can acknowledge it and let it go.

You can become more mindful by connecting to your breath: Clear your mind and breathe. Often in times of stress, we hold our breath. Focusing on your breath will bring you into the present moment. You can use a timer to remind you to breathe deeply. You can count the length of an inhale, and an exhale. You can lengthen your breath. You can think of the words inner on the inhale and peace on the exhale. Repeat breathing cycles to gain mindfulness and presence in the moment. Pay close attention to your breathing, especially when experiencing intense emotions and stress.

Music, dance, and movement make you mindful. Play the music you enjoy in the present moment: Play, dance and sing along. Move your body. Let some of those emotions out through music, song, and movement. Strong emotions such as sadness, anger, or fear make it harder to gain distance. How can you move that anger through your body if you have pent-up outrage? Is it through running, kick boxing or another active sport? Or do you need calming gentleness? Would yoga, tai chi, or calming music help you?

You can become mindful by asking yourself: What am I feeling? What am I needing? What am I wanting? What am I willing to do? Starting your day with these questions is a beautiful way to check in and get honest about your feelings, needs, and wants. Tune into your body's sensations, needs, and desires. Mindfulness is a beautiful way to encourage self-care to foster healing and growth.

Find moments in your day to be mindful and re-set your focus: Try a walking meditation where you take notice and stay present along your walk. Sit in awe outside. Take note of nature. One of my favourite meditations is the Loving Kindness Meditation:

May I be strong. May I be peaceful.
May I be happy. May I be healthy.
May I be safe. May I be wise.

Take as much time as you need to repeat these words. There is plenty of mindfulness meditations available to you. Find as many moments as you can throughout the day to become mindful!

REFLECTION QUESTIONS:

- What brings you into the present moment?
- What type of mindfulness will benefit you?
- How will you practice mindfulness?

HOW TO FOSTER EMOTIONAL AGILITY TO GAIN SELF-AWARENESS

All the emotions you feel, whether good or bad, are signals that will help you navigate through life. Emotional agility is not about ignoring complicated feelings and thoughts. It's about holding them loosely, facing them courageously and compassionately, and then moving past them to bring more peace and strength to your life. Here are some actionable steps to help you understand your emotions and gain emotional agility.

You can pace yourself through these steps when presented with a challenge, stress, or situation that brings up feelings. First, it's about showing up, stepping back, acting out your why, and finally, moving forward. Be patient with yourself, and remember the more you practice, the better you get at this process. The self-awareness that comes with emotional agility is empowering!

Showing up and facing your emotions: This means facing your thoughts, feelings, and behaviours willingly, with curiosity and kindness. Is this an accurate reflection of reality or a harmful distortion? Objectively and non-judgementally, look at what comes to mind for you. Give yourself compassion and permission to be human with your emotions. Please don't hold your feelings too tightly; face them with courage and compassion. Permit yourself to feel these emotions, even if they are tough.

Stepping back and gaining perspective: After facing your thoughts and emotions, it is about detaching from and observing them to see them for what they are. Thoughts are just thoughts, and feelings are just feelings. Detached observations give a broader view of a whole chessboard versus a single piece. You can zoom out your lens as a camera pulls back to view the bigger picture and step away from the drama. Buy yourself some space and time. Tell yourself, "How fascinating!" or "I have to think about this." This perspective will allow you to respond instead of reacting. What might these emotions be telling you? What thoughts have led to these emotions? Is there a better feeling thought that you could have? Is there a thought that would make you feel better? What idea might make you feel better?

Walking your why and your truth: After you've un-cluttered and calmed your mental processes and created space between thoughts and the thinker, you can focus more on your core values and what is most important. Consider things like: How do you want your life to look? How do you deserve to be treated? What might your boundaries be? What do you value and desire in your life? What do you want most for yourself? What are you in control of, and what do you want to change?

Walking your why is about recognizing, accepting, and then distancing yourself from scary, painful, disruptive emotional stuff so that you can connect thinking with feeling and with long-term values and aspirations. This step helps you understand your emotions and what you want for yourself moving forward. It makes sense that you feel angry if you value safety and honesty. This step is about being honest with yourself, getting more clarity on what you love and deserve, and how you want to show up in your life.

Keep moving forward: Take some time to think about your core values and personal goals. What matters to you in life? What situations make you feel good? What kind of relationship would you like to have? If your life became a film, what would it be about? Now, notice if your daily actions support your values and move you closer to your goals. Reconnect to those things, people, and situations that genuinely help you in your desired direction. Define your own life. That is the only thing you have influence over, one foot in front of the other. Keep going!

A JOURNEY THROUGH JOURNALING TO GAIN SELF-AWARENESS.

Let it out. It's tiring to act okay and be strong when you're close to the edge of a breakdown, exhausted and depleted. Stress, confusion and worry can be challenging when you love someone with an addiction. Gaining self-awareness and processing emotions and thoughts becomes essential for your well-being. Acknowledging and confronting difficult emotions allows for healing and brings about a sense of empowerment and the ability to cope with struggle positively. Journaling is a beautiful positive intervention that can help you build resilience.

Journaling is a beautiful tool that can help you become more self-aware. It not only enables you to process your emotions, but it's also like speaking and listening at the same time. Writing in a journal allows you to express your thoughts, feelings, and what is happening around you. It is a method to get the thoughts and feelings out of your head and onto paper to understand them more clearly. Journaling allows you to gain perspective.

Many people confuse journaling with a diary. A diary is a book that records events that have happened. A journal is a book used to express emotions and write out thoughts and ideas. Journaling is shown to ease stress as well as reduce anxiety and depression. One of the best benefits of journaling is that it allows you to gain more self-awareness by cutting through the mental clutter and providing insight. Journaling will enable you to organize your thoughts, process your emotions, and relieve stress.

Self-reflection and self-awareness enhance your ability to honour your feelings, see your thoughts, and reflect on your values. Allow yourself to write freely. Use journaling as an excellent tool to identify things that might be going under the radar in your mind. Journaling is lovely because it's never judgmental and offers clarity and awareness while helping you with direction.

To start journaling, you only need a pen, notebook, or journal. There are no rules or expectations associated with writing in your journal. You can start small and choose to do it at any time. Journaling was one of the most powerful things I did when dealing with my boyfriend in active addiction. Start writing, speak your truth, and allow things to flow naturally without any filter. You will be amazed by how things will flow out of you.

You can use your journal to record events or situations you are presented with or pull out your journal when you have emotions or thoughts you'd like to process. You can use your journal to process positive emotions, celebrate wins, and express negative feelings and thoughts. Don't censor or edit while you write. Let anything and everything come out, even if it's gibberish. Remember, this journal is for your eyes only so that you can be sincere. There is no right way to journal. The key is to use journaling as a tool that will work best for you.

Here are some journal prompts for self-reflection and self-discovery:

- What would I say if I were a fly on the wall and could speak?
- What is most challenging for me at this time is.
- Right now, I feel.
- What's going on for me right now is.
- What makes me happy is.
- If I knew I could not fail, I would.
- What I need to accept is.
- What makes me happy is.
- The last time I felt this way was.
- What's bugging me right now is.
- What do I need to let go of?
- Who do I admire and why?
- The things that I'm most concerned about are.
- My older version of myself would tell me.

- It makes sense that I'm feeling the way I am, considering the situation.
- What can I do in this situation to make me feel better?
- I would rather.

Journaling is a method of expressing and releasing thoughts and feelings. It is a powerful tool for healing that relieves the brain of holding all these experiences and allows you to release tension. As a result of journaling, you will feel better. I resisted journaling for so long, then I started journaling when my mind felt like it would explode, and it was a turning point and game changer for me. Please, give it a try if you haven't already.

REFLECTION QUESTIONS:

- When will you journal?
- How will journaling help you gain self-awareness?

HOW TO CULTIVATE A GROWTH MINDSET TO GAIN SELF-AWARENESS

Renowned Stanford University Psychologist Carol Dweck teaches that your beliefs strongly affect your life.

The growth mindset is based on the assumption that your essential qualities are things you can cultivate through effort. Everyone can change and grow through application and experience. For example, you might think: *"This is hard. I must tap into my strength and figure out how to take my life back."* If you had a fixed mindset, you might think: *"This is terrible. People like me always end up with losers like this. I can't do anything about it."* A fixed mindset limits your potential and ability to grow, evolve, and learn. A growth mindset embraces learning, change, potential, and hope.

The great news is that anyone can cultivate a growth mindset despite the most significant life challenges. When you have gone through challenges and struggles in your life and choose to apply a growth mindset, it is called post-traumatic growth in positive psychology. Mindset can change the meaning you give to circumstances. Mindset changes the meaning of failure and challenge as well. Even with a growth mindset, a loss can be painful. But it doesn't have to define you as a person. You might describe yourself with things like: *"My life sucks,"* *"I'm a bad parent,"* or *"Why do I attract men like this?"* With a growth mindset, you approach a life struggle as a problem to be faced, dealt with, and conquered.

With a fixed mindset, losing oneself to failure can be permanent, haunting, and traumatic, leading to blame, fault finding, making excuses, and eventually not wanting to try. Adopting a growth mindset is empowering as you become a learner who believes you can get better, healthier, and more resilient. Success is about stretching yourself and facing struggle head-on to grow and learn from it. A growth mindset is about becoming resilient, sufficient, and a learner.

The different mindsets become essential when we look at what it means to be resilient. When you're stuck holding a fixed mindset, you are more likely to be judgmental and critical of yourself, others, and situations. When people tend to have more of a growth mindset, they focus on learning and asking questions like: *"How can I learn?"* and *"How can I become better?"* Cultivating curiosity and a growth mindset will enable you to persevere in the face of setbacks and obstacles, support you in valuing effort and personal mastery, keep you open to feedback, learn from others, and many other factors that lead to success. A growth mindset is a prerequisite to stepping into a place of resilience and bouncing back better.

Name That Mindset

See if you can spot the mindset in these statements:

- This means I am a loser.
- This means I'm a terrible wife.
- I look so stupid right now.

- I suck at this.
- Even though this situation is challenging,
- I can figure things out.
- How can I take care of myself?
- Why does this keep happening to me?
- I wonder what it is like to be addicted to drugs.

Map Your Mindset

- Ask yourself:
- Where have you had this black-or-white thinking, all-or-nothing thinking?
- Do you believe that people can learn to improve as they put in more effort?
- When have you had a learning, curious mindset?

Change Your Questions, Change Your Path

The book *Change Your Questions Change Your Life* by Marilee Adams demonstrates two paths: a judger path and a learner path. She says that people think in questions, and we tend to go down the judger path when triggered. She created a choice map, demonstrating that we choose which direction we go down; we can judge or learn. Approach life like you are standing at the beginning of this path, where anything can impact you at any moment (aka trigger), a result of which you will have thoughts, feelings, and circumstances, and you must choose where your mind goes, or, let the mind react by default

The judger path tends to focus on who is to blame. Questions you might ask are: *What's wrong with me? Why am I such a loser? Why are they so dumb?* After a while, we go into what Marilee Adams called the JUDGER PIT, where we stay in the problem.

The learner path tends to focus on opportunities to learn. Questions you might ask are: *What can I do to grow from this situation? What happened? What is useful here? What are the options? What is another way to see this?* You can switch paths at any time. *Change your questions to curiosity-based questions such as: What will I do next? How else can I think about this? What do I need right now?*

Next time you face a challenge, think about how you can shift towards a learner path and see how different and empowering it feels. Ask curious questions. The judger path is problem-focused, and the learner path is solution-focused. Judger's path makes you feel stuck. The learner path keeps you moving forward, working through life circumstances. The judger is a fixed mindset, and the learner is a growth mindset.

Curiosity encourages a growth mindset.

You will naturally find yourself in this upward spiral when you use interest or curiosity as the antidote to a fixed mindset. Ben Zander, the conductor of joy, suggests regularly utilizing the expression *"how fascinating"* to step into a place of curiosity and a growth mindset.

Mindset Path Activity

1. Walk the two paths: Think of recent adversity you encountered using the learner and then the judger paths. Write out the statements that would put you on the judger path. Write out the statements that would put you on the learner's path.

2. Challenge your fixed mindset beliefs. Say things like, "That's not true because..." or ask, "Another way of seeing this is..."

3. Identify your triggers and practice redirecting from the judger path to the learner path.

KEY TAKE-AWAYS

✓ Self-awareness harnesses the power to tap into your mind and constructively honour your emotions, thoughts, and beliefs.

✓ What you continually think about becomes your world. The mind is one of the most substantial, valuable powers you possess.

✓ Regardless of what is going on and how powerless you feel, you influence your thoughts.

✓ Think about self-awareness like you're gaining self-knowledge through emotional exploration and self-management.

✓ All the emotions you feel, good or bad, are signals that will help you navigate through life. Emotional agility is not about ignoring complicated feelings and thoughts. It's about holding them loosely, facing them courageously and compassionately.

✓ You can build self-awareness through mindfulness, adopting a growth mindset, and journaling.

CHAPTER REFLECTION QUESTIONS:

Take a moment to write down your highlights from this chapter:

- What takeaways are going to inspire you the most going forward?

_____

_____

_____

_____

_____

_____

- What brought a significant or slight shift in your thinking, feelings, or behaviour?

_____

_____

_____

_____

_____

_____

CHAPTER THREE

You Are Lovable:
Leveraging Positivity Using Appreciation and Gratitude to Gain Your Footing

"Every day may not be good, but there is something good in every day." — Adage.

You are lovable and don't allow anyone to make you feel like you are hard to love. I felt like this when I was in the heart of my partner's active addiction. I started to question my worth and lovability. Sometimes it might be hard to see the good, the positive, and your strengths, especially when knocked down by someone else's addiction, but you can adopt a habit of hunting for the good stuff. To regain your power, it becomes imperative to safeguard your mental health and well-being by appreciating and noticing what is good. You can find glimmers of hope in some of the most challenging times.

Casting all your concern onto and tending to others' struggles sometimes causes you to lose sight of who you are and what is good. This external focus and worry can lead to a downward spiral. Dr. Robert Emmons and many leading scholars in the positive psychology movement emphasize the impact and power of gratitude for your well-being and resilience. They teach that you can cultivate gratitude and embrace all the benefits it brings to your life. There is power in harnessing the process of appreciating yourselves and being grateful for your natural talents, strengths, and gifts.

In this chapter, you will discover the following:
- What are self-appreciation and gratitude?
- Why self-appreciation and gratitude are essential when embracing your power.
- How to leverage positivity to bring more joy and happiness.
- How to turn on the strength spotting switch.
- How to use self-appreciation and gratitude to increase positivity.
- What hope is, who it's for and how it helps regain your power.

WHAT EXACTLY IS GRATITUDE?

Generally, the concept is when you are grateful, acknowledge that you have received a gift, recognize the value of the gift, and appreciate the donor's intention. Gratitude is pleasing, it feels good, and it is also motivating. When you feel grateful, you are moved to share goodness with others. Appreciation acts as a spotlight on the good.

When you go through the challenges and struggles of loving someone with an addiction, gratitude and appreciation become excellent tools to help you regain hope for a better future and feel better in the present. Although finding the good in the challenge might be hard, there is always something good alongside struggle. Gratitude is the emotion that can help you see and savour the good.

Practicing Gratitude Makes You Happier

A sense of wonder, thankfulness, and appreciation is likely to elevate happiness for several reasons:

1. Grateful thinking fosters the savouring of positive life experiences and situations.

2. People extract the maximum possible satisfaction and enjoyment from their circumstances.

3. Counting blessings may directly counteract the effects of hedonic adaptation, the process by which your happiness level returns again and again to its set point. Counting your blessings prevents people from taking their lives for granted.

4. The very act of seeing things as a gift is likely beneficial for mood.

5. Gratitude strengthens social ties.

6. It is good for relationships and marriage.

7. Gratitude affects your heart rhythms.

8. Gratitude enhances your human spirit. It adds meaning and purpose to your life.

Gratitude is recognizing and acknowledging the goodness in one's life. Gratitude is more than a feeling. Gratitude is not just a form of "positive thinking" or a technique of "Happiology," how to be happy all the time, but rather a deep recognition and acknowledgment that goodness exists under even the worst that life has to offer. Gratitude and appreciation are chosen attitudes, life approaches, and conscious decisions that build hope. You can sharpen your ability to recognize and acknowledge the giftedness of life.

Gratitude is such a powerful emotion, one that can make your life better. It is difficult to feel stressed, overwhelmed, and sorry for yourself while simultaneously feeling grateful and good about yourself. Sometimes when your world feels chaotic and out of control, it becomes easy to feel defeated and deflated. Gratitude, appreciation and hope are beautiful emotions that can shift you to a better place.

According to gratitude researchers Emmon and Mc-Cullough, gratitude can:

- Help to make friends.
- Improve your physical health.
- Improve your psychological health.
- Enhance empathy.
- Reduce aggression.
- Improve your sleep.
- Improve your self-esteem.
- Increase mental strength.

SELF-APPRECIATION AND GRATITUDE: THE INGREDIENTS TO REGAIN YOUR POWER

"Keep taking time for yourself until you're you again."
— *Lalah Delia*

When life seems bleak and challenging, you might wonder, will I be happy again? Do you ever wonder where happiness comes from and how to build more joy? Sonja Lyubomirsky created the happiness pie that addresses the three primary factors influencing life satisfaction or happiness. In the pie chart, 50% is genetic, 10% accounts for circumstances, and 40% is intentional activities or things you can do. The person you love with an addiction is a circumstance that only accounts for 10% of your life satisfaction. In other words, you influence your life with intentional behaviours. You can significantly affect your well-being for the positive. This information is empowering.

People regularly choose behaviours that raise their happiness levels all the time. Faithfully following a yoga practice can boost one's mood and vitality. You might garden, listen to music, hike in nature, write in a journal, shop, or eat chocolate to elevate your mood. These are all examples of intentional behaviours.

Gratitude and appreciation are two intentional behaviours that can influence your level of happiness. Gratitude brings the most joyful, positive emotions to humans. I know sometimes it is tough to find the "good" when pulled down into the pit of addiction, but it is possible. Studies on daily gratitude interventions have shown their positive impact on levels of resilience and well-being, even amidst some of the biggest challenges. An attitude of gratitude and the impact of gratitude interventions have been studied. Its impact on psychological and physical well-being is extraordinary and powerful evidence supporting gratitude.

REFLECTION QUESTIONS:

- What are some intentional behaviours you already do to enhance your well-being?
- Gratitude and appreciation are essential; where are you already practicing these intentional behaviours?

WHAT IS SELF-APPRECIAITON?

If you think about it, what do you do when you appreciate someone for their actions or who they are? Self-appreciation is about turning the kindness that you give to others inward. Just like you appreciate others, self-appreciation is the process of valuing yourself. It's about being grateful for the person you are, the talents you bring, and the strength you possess. Self-appreciation is about consciously acknowledging the positive within you without comparing yourself to others. It is an overall sense of your value and your worth. It's about how you feel about your abilities and your limitations.

One of the best ways to increase your understanding of self-worth and positive emotions is to cultivate self-appreciation. You might sometimes feel that no one sees your value, and then you begin to wonder if you have any value. Do you ever think you're not a good parent, wife, or child because they reject you? Criticism, problems, difficulties, or even setbacks can make you feel like you're not good enough or didn't do enough.

When you love someone who is addicted, you often get under-appreciated. You begin to question yourself and your worth. All too often, the turmoil, manipulation, and lies begin to break you down psychologically. It's in everyone's nature to want to be loved, accepted and appreciated. It becomes essential to build up your self-appreciation, especially when you do not receive it from the people around you. Appreciation starts from within; it is about reflecting on how you are feeling about yourself.

The great news is you can cultivate self-appreciation, and you have access to it at any time.

In their book, *The Power of Appreciation*, Noelle Nelson, Ph.D., and Jennine Lemare Calaba, Psych.D., talk about how research confirms that when people feel appreciated, good things happen to their minds, hearts, and bodies. They explain appreciation as the energy of valuing and being grateful for what you bring to this world. The two components of appreciation are

- Gratitude - you feel or express gratitude, and
- Valuing - actively use your mind and consciously choose to love people, yourself, or things.

REFLECTION QUESTIONS:

- How can you actively choose to love yourself?
- How are you grateful for yourself?
- What do you value about yourself?

THE ENERGY OF APPRECIATION

All life is energy and manifests as vibrations. Science has shown that appreciation changes your vibration. Masaru

Emoto was a Japanese businessman, author and pseudo-scientist who claimed that human consciousness could affect the molecular structure of water. Dr. Emoto's water crystalline structure research demonstrates how appreciation has a powerful effect on energy frequency and how your thoughts, feelings, and music affects water structure. Love, gratitude, and appreciation created and formed beautiful crystals.

Conversely, the energy of hate created distorted and imploded crystals. Words and appreciation affected the structure of water! Why is this important? Your body is made up mostly of water! Candace Pert is a brilliant molecular biologist widely regarded as the mother of a new field of science known as psychoneuroimmunology. In the book *Molecules of Emotions*, Dr. Perts' research in molecular biochemistry demonstrates that appreciation has been scientifically proven to positively affect your heart rate, brain function, and overall well-being.

Appreciation is good energy

According to self-compassion expert Dr. Kristen Neff, self-appreciation is the flip side of or close relative to self-compassion. Sometimes it's more challenging to see what's right about yourself than wrong. At times it can even be hard to think about your positive traits. Compliments and praise are sometimes very hard to accept.

All too often, it's easy to underplay your good points, and you might have a habit of putting yourself down. Hate harms your well-being. Appreciation and self-gratitude can positively impact our well-being.

REFLECTION QUESTIONS:

- Reflection questions:
- How can you healthily recognize your positive qualities?
- Why is it important to do this for yourself right now?

BECOMING AN APPRECIATOR

Appreciation takes courage, considerable resolve, and commitment. It can be extra challenging when you love someone with an addiction as you are dealing with someone that is not thinking straight and will not hesitate to use you, manipulate you, and try to break you down; it's the nature of addiction. But you have the power to do the work of self-appreciation for yourself.

First: Take notice of what you are grateful for already. Start by appreciating life itself. It is beneficial to start the appreciation with things outside yourself first as a form of training:

- Become opportunity-minded instead of problem-minded.
- Develop an appreciative state of mind: Remind yourself to appreciate! Even if you have to put a sign up in your bathroom or car.
- Try thinking thankful thoughts and pessimistic thoughts at the same time. It's okay to be upset and appreciate yourself as well.
- Play appreciative games: find as many things to value as possible.
- Deepen appreciation for others: consider how you value friends, spouses, kids, dogs, etc.

Second: Turn appreciation towards yourself. This focus can be challenging, but it can powerfully shift your vibration and energy:

- Weed out negative beliefs,
- Catch your inner voice when it lacks appreciation,
- Explore good qualities and values, and be grateful for them.
- Think about and write down all the things you appreciate about yourself.
- Keep that value list visible for you to see and read.
- Read it every day and when you feel down. Keep growing the list.

- Add it to your list when someone compliments you, and savour the gesture.

PRACTICE APPRECIATION AND GRATITUDE

Gratitude is about noticing good things, looking for them, and appreciating them. It's about savouring, absorbing, and paying attention to those things. Some of the best ways to practice gratitude are to express your appreciation for yourself, write it down, or thank someone. There are many ways to practice gratitude and appreciation. You can try one or more of the following suggestions and see how it makes you feel.

Simple ways to practice gratitude:

- Keep a gratitude journal.
- Think about what you are grateful for often.
- Stop and take notice.
- Savour and stretch out the things for which you are thankful.
- Adopt a sense of wonder.
- Practice continual thankfulness.
- Come to your senses - what do I taste, see, smell, hear, or feel?
- Make gratitude reminders.

- Gratitude ABCs - Find something to be grateful for with each letter of the alphabet.
- Embrace challenges as hidden opportunities.
- Look for situations to flex your gratitude muscles.
- Tell people thank you verbally or in writing.
- Nurture the friendships that you have.
- Smile more often.
- Include acts of kindness in your life each day.
- Avoid gossiping or speaking badly about another person.
- Gratitude walk - walk and savour the good in your life.
- Meditate with your gratitude list.
- Dinner grace with gratitude.
- Count your blessings daily.
- Be mindful and stay in the present moment.
- Say thank you even for the minor things in your life.
- Take notice of even a tiny blessing.
- When you have a negative thought, try to see growth opportunities.
- Write a thank you letter or text to someone.
- When times are bad, lean on your friends for support.
- Share the good things that are happening in your life.
- Incorporate gratitude into your prayers.
- Focus on your strengths.

- Gratitude Rock reminder. Find a rock and write the word gratitude on it.
- Spend quality time with people that make you feel good.
- No matter how tough things get, limit your worry time.

Appreciating Yourself

List ten things about yourself that you like or appreciate. As you write down each quality, see if you notice any uncomfortable feelings of embarrassment, fear, vanity, or unfamiliarity. If any discomfort arises, remind yourself that you are not claiming that you're better than anyone else or that you're perfect. You're merely noting the good qualities that you possess.

POSITIVITY: YOUR FUEL FOR RESILIENCE

The main reason gratitude and appreciation enhance your well-being is that fuel that generates an upward spiral of positivity that feels good. Some might ask if positivity is putting on a smile or burying your head in the sand and pretending nothing is challenging going on around you.

What is positivity?

It is probably not surprising that positivity is central to positive psychology. Positivity doesn't always mean simply smiling and looking cheerful; however, positivity is more about one's overall perspective and tendency to focus on all that is good. Positivity is the practice or preference to be positive or optimistic in life. When you are positive, you engage in positive thinking, emotions, and behaviours like kindness and generosity.

As described earlier in this book, positive psychology is the scientific study of human flourishing. It focuses on the positive events and influences in life, including positive experiences like happiness, joy, inspiration, and love. Also, positivity focuses on positive states and traits like gratitude, resilience, and compassion. It is not a "happiology" or study of how to be happy always.

Positivity emphasizes the positive influences each one of us has in our life. These include character strengths, optimistic emotions, and constructive institutions. Positivity is the belief that happiness is derived from emotional and mental factors and that you influence your own happiness.

The health benefits of positivity may include and are not limited to the following:

- Increased life span.
- Lower rates of depression and suicide.
- Lower levels of distress and pain.
- Greater resistance to illnesses.
- Better psychological and physical well-being.
- Better cardiovascular health and reduced risk of death from cardiovascular disease and stroke.
- Reduced risk of death from cancer.
- Reduced risk of death from respiratory conditions.
- Reduced risk of death from infections.
- Better coping skills during hardships and stress.

What is toxic positivity?

It is prevalent to strive towards a happy life, and the message often received is to "be positive." Our positivity culture in Western society may be toxic positivity which harms individuals and communities. "Think positive!" If only it were that simple. Toxic positivity is the excessive and ineffective overgeneralization of a happy, optimistic state surrounding all situations. Toxic positivity can be damaging, resulting in denial, minimization, and invalidation of authentic human emotions. And ironically, the constant pressure to be positive can make you feel even worse.

It is impossible to be positive and happy all the time.

When someone is struggling, the last thing they need is pressure to "be positive." You are no exception. When referring to positivity, I am not referring to the belief that people should put a positive spin on all experiences, even those profoundly tragic or traumatizing ones. Toxic positivity can silence negative emotions, demean grief, and make people feel under pressure to pretend to be happy even when they are struggling. The term fake it until you make it is a term that could be unhelpful and even hurtful.

Given my education and immersion in positive psychology, I remember imposing toxic positivity onto myself, telling myself to move on or look for a positive in my loss while actively grieving. First, I needed to honour my emotions while grieving and healing. Toxic positivity imposes positive thinking as the only solution to problems, demanding that a person avoid negative thinking or expressing negative emotions. Of course, as I talk about positivity, gratitude and appreciation, these are alongside challenges and not invalidating the struggle, grief and loss that you might be going through.

Some of the risks involved with toxic positivity are:

- Isolating yourself.
- Stigma.
- Shaming.
- Demeaning emotions.
- Ignoring grief and sadness.
- Lack of communication.
- Self-judgement.
- Ignoring actual harm or dangers.
- Burying emotions.

Is it okay to be negative? As mentioned in the previous chapter, humans feel a wide range of emotions, each of which is an essential part of well-being. Not acknowledging these emotions means ignoring the action they can inspire. Although positivity, gratitude and self-appreciation offer many benefits, no one can always be positive. Positivity can exist alongside challenge and is the key to thriving during adversity and has been shown to boost resilience. Here are some strategies to help you avoid toxic positivity. Feel your feelings and practice radical acceptance.

Some strategies for avoiding toxic positivity include:

- recognizing negative emotions as normal and an essential part of the human experience

- identifying and naming emotions rather than trying to avoid them
- talking with trusted people about emotions, including negative feelings
- seeking support from nonjudgmental people, such as a trusted friend, coaches, clergyperson, support groups, or a Therapist
- When someone tells you about their problem, listen, really listen. Acknowledge their pain. You can say, "That is so hard," or "I'm sorry you're going through this."
- When you are struggling, listen, really listen to yourself. Acknowledge your pain. You can say to yourself, "That is so hard," or "I'm sorry I'm going through this."
- Practice radical acceptance and "feel your feelings." Accept reality. You are no longer in denial or desperately trying to downplay or suppress things.

The pressure to "think positive" is harmful because it leads to feelings of guilt and emotional repression. While positivity can help people deal with difficult times, toxic positivity does the opposite. While people can find comfort in positivity, toxic positivity leads to someone's emotions being dismissed, ignored or invalidated. Positivity is different than just "thinking positive" and can be very powerful to help you regain your power. Positivity is being positive or optimistic in life, even alongside challenges. It is hopefulness and confidence about the future or the successful outcome of something.

Positivity is the quality of being full of hope, emphasizing the good parts of a situation, not ignoring the struggles or challenging emotions, and believing that something good will happen in some form or another.

Research from the field of positive psychology shows that when you are positive, you are more engaged, creative, motivated, energetic, resilient, and productive. Shawn Achor is an American author and speaker known for his advocacy of positive psychology. He authored *The Happiness Advantage* and founded *GoodThink*. Achor calls the benefits of positivity "the happiness advantage" because your brain performs better when positive than when negative, neutral, or stressed.

THE UPWARD SPIRAL OF POSITIVE EMOTIONS

In her book Positivity, positivity researcher Dr. Barbara Fredrickson talks about the power of a three-to-one ratio, where you must have three positive emotions for every negative emotion. If you can do this, it will help you to be more resilient and bounce back better. The ratio means that for every heart-wrenching negative emotional experience you endure, you experience at least three heartfelt positive emotional experiences that uplift you. She reveals that this three-to-one ratio is ideal for building your survival and thriving mind. It is important to note that this is not about just pretending bad things don't happen or denying the reality of situations.

Positivity needs to be more pervasive and consists of various positive emotions, such as love, joy, amusement, gratitude, and hope. Improving the positive-to-negative emotion ratio is essential for our well-being, resilience, and happiness. There are strategies and practices that you can do to increase these positive emotions. Dr. Fredrickson encourages everyone to tap into the potential for life-giving positivity even amidst some of your biggest challenges.

INCREASE POSITIVITY WITH GRATITUDE JOURNALING

Journaling or writing down a few things you are grateful for is one of the easiest ways to practice gratitude. Journaling allows you to reflect on your day and helps you to remember the good things. You can enhance gratitude's effectiveness by focusing on all the good things that happened to you in a given time. Staying with this positive emotion is tremendously vital for your well-being. When you go through a struggle, getting wrapped up in the negative emotions that come with it is common and easy.

Journaling is a fantastic tool and practice that will help you express your gratitude and enhance positive emotions. You can return to your journal's previous entries when things seem bleak or challenging. Journaling is also powerful for helping you express and process feelings. You could journal out some complicated emotions and then move into a place of gratitude and acceptance.

Instead of just identifying what you are grateful for, try to dig into why you are thankful.

Gratitude Journal Prompts:
I am grateful for my courage because

_____

Three good things that happened to me this week were

_____

I am grateful for my friendships because

_____

Something else I am grateful for is

_____

I am grateful for my family because

_____

I am grateful for who I am because

_____

How can I rewrite the story that my negativity bias might be telling me

_____

What opportunities might be in this difficulty

_____

What would it look like if I overestimated my ability to overcome challenges

_____

NEGATING THE NEGATIVITY BIAS

The negativity bias is a cognitive bias that explains why adverse events or feelings typically have a more significant impact on our psychological state than positive events or feelings, even when they are of equal proportion. Humans are wired to notice the harmful or life-threatening things in their lives. The negativity bias is a built-in system to keep us safe.

It's natural to ignore one's blessings or even complain about them. You are evolutionarily wired to see the negative. As a human, you want to be emotionally and intellectually healthy, but thanks to evolution, you have a negative bias that makes you notice what's wrong instead of right. Most people are blind to strengths and therefore miss the potential they might have for us during challenging times.

According to psychologist Dr. Rick Hanson, the brain is like Velcro (or sticky) for negative experiences but like a Teflon pan (or slippery) for positive ones. Everyone has challenging times and many emotional struggles when we love someone with an addiction, and it can be hard to stay positive with such complex challenges. First, your emotions are valid and okay. Still, the negativity bias might add insult to injury because it overestimates the threat of situations and might underestimate our ability to manage these threats. Negativity has a longer shelf life, so to speak, and is a rigid wired design in our nervous system. Being aware of the negativity bias is an excellent place to start. Then, tapping into your ability to offset the tendency to be negative becomes key to regaining your power.

REFLECTION QUESTIONS:

- Where might you have a negativity bias?
- How does the negativity bias show up for you?

Transforming Negativity

The next time you find yourself in the grip of negative emotions, try generating positive feelings alongside them. For example,

It's hard to feel _____ (fill in the blank) right now. Feeling _____ (fill in the blank) is part of the human experience.

What can I do to make myself happier at this moment?

In her compelling book, Broken Open, Elizabeth Lesser says, "Suffering and crisis transform us, humble us, and bring out what matters most in life." You can try as you may, but you can't control how life goes. The unexpected and undesired happen every day. Yet when you wrap your suffering in the cocoon of compassion, something new emerges, something excellent, exquisite, and beautiful, much like a butterfly. By changing the way you relate to your imperfections and pain, you can change your living experience. Use positive emotions to change suffering into joy.

Seeing possibilities and challenging your beliefs about your limitations to become more hopeful for a better future for yourself can help you regain your power. One of the best ways to transform the negativity bias is to practice gratitude and appreciation to make those positive emotions stick around longer. I always say it's like squeezing every last bit of juice out of a juicy orange and savouring the goodness.

THE PARADOX OF HAPPINESS AND SUFFERING

In essence, the journey is about surrendering to a difficult time, acknowledging it and honouring it, which leads to an understanding and transformation. Subjective well-being states that most people are happy. Research suggests that gratitude is the ingredient that keeps us going despite trying and challenging times. Through the process of appreciation, what was once taken for granted is now seen as unique. For example, there is nothing quite like the potential or actual unavailability of something or someone to make us value it more in the case of loss.

Since our brains are wired to see the harmful and potential harm to keep us safe, it can be tough to be optimistic, grateful, and hopeful. The bounce-back factor is an essential ingredient to thriving in challenging situations. The paradox is that the grateful outlook on life offers protection in times of crisis, but it is challenging to practice appreciation and gratitude amongst struggle. Gratitude provides overall resiliency across a lifespan. Resiliency is the ability to spring back from and successfully adapt to adversity.

The other part of the paradox is that you tend to reach out for support when you are suffering. This support offers human connection, belief in humanity and optimism, which is shown to contribute to happiness. Optimism transforms helplessness into possibility. The results of studies on well-being and good relationships, optimism is one of the best predictors of happiness. Social support changes how you view challenges and how equipped you to feel about tackling them.

When you go through a struggle, you will learn and grow. You gain growth opportunities, a sense of accomplishment and learning from struggle, which all contribute to your well-being. It is a paradox as you need the challenges in life for all this growth to occur.

Stanford health psychologist Dr. Kelly McGonigal reveals that your perceptions about stress are more important than how much stress you experience. Reframe stress as a challenge rather than a threat. Knowing the paradox of happiness and struggle does not make what you might be going through any less damaging, but the awareness might help you see alongside the fight some goodness.

REFLECTION QUESTIONS:

- How can you be more positive and resilient during challenging times?
- How can you reframe stress as a challenge rather than a threat?

HUNT FOR YOUR GOOD STUFF

In the book *Flourish*, the father of positive psychology, Martin Seligman, suggests thinking about and journaling the following:
- What went well?
- Three good things.
- What are your superpowers?

- What makes you, you?
- How would your mom, best friend, or co-worker that loves you, describe you? If you can't think of it, ask them what they admire about you.

Go on the hunt for all the things that make you lovable. Keep a file or journal and add to it every day.

TURNING ON THE STRENGTH SWITCH

When times get tough, recall your hard-earned strengths and tell yourself you're up for the challenge.

There is power in using and knowing your strengths. In the *Strength Switch*, Lea Waters, Ph.D., teaches you to focus on what is "right" about yourself instead of "wrong." The *Strength Switch* is about instilling positivity to build the foundation that protects you from the anxiety and depression almost inevitable when you love someone with an addiction. She teaches about the negativity bias and why it is crucial to break through it to boost self-esteem and improve your well-being.

Dr. Lea Waters says strengths are positive qualities that energize you, that you perform well and choose often. Doing those activities that seem to come easy to you and lift you up. When you practice and appreciate your strengths, you can use them to help you reach goals, get through the crisis, and even help with personal development. The strength switch is the tool you can use to short-circuit negative thoughts. It is a mental switch to turn on to help you shift your attention from weaknesses to strengths. Your strengths are always here, but they might be hiding. It becomes essential to appreciate and honour your strengths to regain your power.

Flipping the switch is like turning on the spotlight so you can see and find your strengths. Turn the spotlight off the negative and shine a light on the positive. As mentioned earlier, you have a negative default (or bias) and long-standing issues that cause you to react. Where attention goes, energy flows. The more you focus and talk about the struggle in your life, the more that challenge consumes you. Conversely, the more you comment on success, the more likely you will act successfully. By flipping the switch or putting a spotlight to focus on your power, you will rewire your brain and feel more powerful.

Knowing your strengths and appreciating them with gratitude can help you rewire your brain. You feel more secure and worthy when you value yourself and practice self-appreciation. By appreciating yourself, you tap into your strengths, skills, and ability to handle what life throws at you with greater confidence.

REFLECTION QUESTIONS:

- What will help you flip the switch?
- What are your strengths you can appreciate?
- Where do you want to shine the spotlight?

Find Your Strengths

Think of a time you were at your best:

- What did you do?
- How did it feel?
- What impact did it have on others?

Write down as many strengths you can think of that you have. Finding your strengths is tricky since you sometimes need the language for strengths. As a clue, strengths can be skills, abilities, interests, characteristics, traits, or talents. According to Dr. Lea Waters, strengths have three key elements:

- Performance (being good at something).
- Energy (feeling good doing it).
- High use (choosing to do it).

REFLECTION QUESTIONS:

- What are you good at?
- What feels good for you to do?
- What do you choose to do often?
- What strengths did you use today?

Assess Your Strengths

When moving toward your strengths, consider taking a strength quiz. You can generate your profile at www.viacharacter.org, where over seven million people have taken the VIA Survey. The examination reveals your signature strengths or your best self's top strengths.

An excellent way to describe signature strengths is that they likely involve the "three E's."

- Essential: The strengths are core to who you are.
- Energizing: The strengths are uplifting and give you a boost of energy or joy.
- Effortless: The strengths come easily and naturally to you—you can use them without effort.

Build Your Strengths

Learn how to direct your attention away from weaknesses and towards strengths, sustain attention in focused ways to build strengths through practice, and learn from experiences. Build your strengths by:

Building Attention: Reframe activities from struggle to opportunity. Build directed attention through savouring, gratitude, and mindfulness!

Savouring: Practice enjoyable forms of attention training that capture the moments of good experiences. Build a bank account of "goodness." Savouring helps train attentional skills and boosts happiness, positive mood, and life satisfaction. Savour the good! Exaggerate and take advantage of goodness.

Gratitude: Gratitude is about noticing and actively appreciating the good things in your life. There is a cascade of neurochemistry that good feelings bring.

LET STRESS UNLEASH YOUR CHARACTER STRENGTH

Transform stress into positive personal growth! Chronic stress is a severe problem when you love someone with an addiction. Whether you're going through a huge life event like divorce, a painful loss, or just struggling with minor daily hassles, there's no escaping stress. Thankfully, you can change the way you respond to these stressors. One of the best things you can do is nurture these strengths. Use strengths to create better-coping strategies, build stronger relationships, improve overall health, and increase happiness.

In *The Upside of Stress*, scientist Dr. Kelly McGonigal reviews a massive amount of stress research and points out that "the most common effects of stress include strengths, growth, and resilience." She breaks these down into the five most commonly reported positive changes that people experience following a loss, trauma, or life challenge:

1. A sense of personal strength
2. Increased appreciation for life
3. Spiritual growth
4. Enhanced social connections and relationships with others
5. Identifying new possibilities and life directions.

Now consider the situation from a positive/growth angle.

What did you learn from this experience?

How did it help you in some way? As you answer, consider each of the five positive changes that often result from stress.

When faced with a stressful situation, tap into your strengths from previous challenges.

- What have you overcome that you're proud of?
- What did you learn from it?
- What quality or strength propels you through?
- How can you use your strengths now?

Stress Can Unleash Character Strengths

Let's look more closely at the term "character strengths." Character strengths are positive parts of your personality that define you and help you reach favourable outcomes, they make up what is best for you. When you are at your best, your character strengths are right there, helping you along the way. When you are suffering, overcome by stress, facing difficult emotions, or lost in an argument with a loved one, you can unleash your character strengths.

Stress is generally thought of as evil, something harmful that hurts us. This fixed mindset around stress is because stress has gotten a bad rap over the years. Chronic stress and poor coping are connected with bad health, worsening relationships, decreased concentration, and other harmful effects.

The Upside of Stress.

Can Stress Really Be Something Positive? Stress is a fundamental requirement for growth. The narrowing effect of stress works like this. When stress has a hold, your attention begins to narrow and hyperfocus. This is your brain's attempt to drill down to the problem at hand and try fixing it. In the book, The Stregths-Based Workbook for Stress Relief, Dr. Ryan Niemiec breaks down what he calls the "positivity of stress" into two levels: eustress and motivating distress.

Eustress refers to good or positive stress—something that causes some upset, concern, or worry but is ultimately a favourable or positive stressor. Examples include preparing for your child's birthday party, taking a family vacation, retiring, moving into a new home, or getting promoted at work. Consider some areas of your life that you know are positive and enjoyable but also cause some stress for you. List a few here.

_____

_____

_____

_____

_____

_____

_____

_____

_____

_____

Motivating Distress This second category of positive stress turns our distress (negative stressors) into useful, beneficial, or meaningful stress. Any worry, conflict, or problem you have can also become an opportunity to learn, motivate, improve, or help others. Motivating distress may not remove the worry, but it offers another equally true perspective: when one door closes, another is being opened.

Reflecting on past successes, writing them down, and sharing them with others can remind you of your ability to handle difficult things. Reflection encourages you to focus on the significance of what you learned from the experience and how you can grow while tapping into your resilience. Shifting your mindset around the different kinds of stress and seeing the possibility of positive stress will enhance your resilience.

REFLECTION QUESTIONS:

- When have you experienced motivating distress, and what doors were opened by these challenges?
- When have you experienced eustress?

HAPPINESS AND STRENGTHS AS ANOTHER PATH TO FEELING GOOD

Study after study, encompassing different groups of people, began to show that five specific character strengths are most aligned with happiness, even generating more happiness:

- Zest—feeling energetic and full of vitality
- Hope—feeling optimistic and focused on the future.
- Love—feeling warm and being closely connected to others.
- Gratitude—feeling appreciative and expressing thanks regularly.
- Curiosity—feeling interested and wanting to explore new topics and situations.

Happiness strengths, all of which reside within you, serve as another pathway for you to build your resilience and happiness. You can see the influential role that these strengths can offer you. This chapter has already discussed gratitude, appreciation and love, and tapping into your strengths.

THE POWERFUL POSITIVE EMOTION OF HOPE

One of the most important things to realize about the emotion of hope is that hope is for you and a better future for yourself. Hope is entirely for you and no one else. You may say, "I hope they get sober," or "I hope they realize how much their addiction is destroying their life." Many people struggle with sadness and hopelessness, especially in a relationship with someone with an addiction. Learning to be hopeful can help you untangle from rumination. This will allow you to shift your perspective to the present moment. Thus you can start visualizing, anticipating, and imagining your future through a more positive lens.

Hopelessness is a feeling of despair or lack of hope that life can feel better than it does. Although hopelessness often includes distress, it also describes a set of beliefs about the world, the future, and your abilities. These feelings may make you pull back from your life and avoid doing things you usually enjoy or being with people you love. It is common to feel hopeless when you are on the rollercoaster of addiction, often because you are placing your hope on another person's behaviour. Once the addiction dictates their behaviour, they again let you down, leaving you hopeless. You are hopeless because you are out of control over their behaviour. But what if you turned that hope back onto you and your own life?

Hope gives you the required energy to change for the better. Hope is your most treasured emotional asset. Hope brings you the motivation and emotional backbone to grow, such as perseverance from life's difficulties. In the book *Learned Hopefulness*, Dan Tomasulo, Ph.D., teaches us how to cultivate hope as a beautiful strength-based tool to overcome depression, challenge, and anxiety. In his book, he talks about how Pandora opened the box and released all the difficulties into the world; she closed it before hope could escape. The story teaches that hope lived amongst all disappointments and pain. Thus, hope became familiar or profoundly experienced them.

Hope is the one positive emotion that can co-exist and is activated when experiencing other challenging negative emotions. To have hope is to cherish a desire with anticipation. Hope can be a desire for something to happen; this can be a wish for the situation to change for the better, as well as a particular dream or aspiration. Hope only works for you and your future since that is the only thing you can control.

Use hope to help you deal with all your difficulties, struggles, and challenges when loving someone with an addiction. Of all the positive emotions, hope is the only one that involves the activation of uncertainty or negativity, which makes hope strikingly or significantly unique

Hopefulness is a powerful positive emotion that can help you regain your power. Hopefulness is not about being Pollyannaish or excessively optimistic but wise. Tomasulo doesn't tell you to ignore the reality of your suffering; he teaches you how to restore balance by increasing awareness and reframing your future. By refocusing on the positive potential that already lies within, you will restore a greater sense of hope than you ever thought was possible. Hope is about focusing on what can be done. Rather than focusing on what's happening or occurred in the past.

Hope springs from uncertainty or negativity like the lotus flower springing from the mud. Hope is a cousin to optimism. Hope is the only positive emotion that needs negativity or uncertainty. Like optimism, hope creates a positive mood about an expectation, a goal, or a future situation. When you are hopeful, you believe that the desired event or circumstance is possible. You can cultivate or learn hopefulness.

Cultivate Hopefulness

1. Take a moment to stop and think about how hopeful or hopeless you are about your future.

2. Rate this on a scale of 1 to 10 (one = completely hopeless, ten = very hopeful).

3. Take about 10 minutes to walk yourself through these possibilities:

   - **Adjust perception:** Transform negative beliefs into hopeful ones.
   - **Shaping feelings:** Cultivate positive emotions. Exploring strengths: Discover your best character qualities to improve your life.
   - **Creating micro-goals:** Set goals calibrated to motivate you. Set goals that don't feel overwhelming and can easily be accomplished and completed.
   - **Finding purpose:** Develop life priorities and determine what matters to you.
   - **Cherishing relationships:** Connect to others and learn how to give and receive.

4. Finally, reaccess and evaluate how your hopefulness score changes after doing this exercise.

The purpose of gratitude, appreciation and hopefulness training is to allow you to realize and appreciate the good in your life, even when your world seems out of control and full of turmoil. Tapping into these powerful emotions is essential to help you regain your power. It can make you realize that every day may not be good, but there is something good in every day.

KEY TAKE-AWAYS

- When you go through the challenges and struggles of loving someone with an addiction, gratitude and appreciation become excellent tools to help you regain hope for a better future and feel better in the present.

- Gratitude is such a powerful emotion, one that can make your life better. It is difficult to feel stressed, overwhelmed, and sorry for yourself while simultaneously feeling grateful and good about yourself.

- Self-appreciation is about turning the kindness that you give to others inward.

- Positivity is the practice or preference to be positive or optimistic in life. Positivity is the quality of being full of hope, emphasizing the good parts of a situation, and not ignoring the struggles or challenging emotions.

- When you practice and appreciate your strengths, you can use them to help you reach goals, get through the crisis, and even help with personal development.

- Hope is a positive emotion that requires negativity or uncertainty. Hope gives you the required energy to change for the better.

CHAPTER REFLECTION QUESTIONS:

Take a moment to write down your highlights from this chapter:

- What takeaways are going to inspire you the most going forward?

_____

_____

_____

_____

_____

_____

- What brought a significant or slight shift in your thinking, feelings, or behaviour?

_____

_____

_____

_____

_____

_____

CHAPTER FOUR

Give Yourself a Break:
Learn Self-Compassion and Be Kind to Yourself

"This is a moment of suffering. Suffering is part of life.
May I be kind to myself in this moment.
May I give myself the compassion I need."
— Kristin Neff

There is a great deal of power in being kind to yourself. When you feel like the world is against you and someone you love is slipping away to addiction like sand between your fingers, being warm and understanding to yourself is essential for empowerment and healing. You build your ability to cope by giving yourself support and encouragement rather than being cold and judgmental when challenges and difficulties arise.

Turning towards understanding, acceptance, and inward love can help you regain your power when suffering, hurting, or feeling knocked down. Research indicates that self-compassion is one of the most potent sources of coping and resilience that can be cultivated and radically improve our mental and physical well-being.

In this chapter, you will understand

- What self-compassion is and why it is essential to regain your power.
- How to use self-compassion for healing and empowerment.
- How to use specific tools to foster more self-compassion.

WHAT IS SELF-COMPASSION?

Self-compassion researcher Kristin Neff indicates that self-compassion is strongly associated with psychological well-being. Higher levels of self-compassion are linked to increased feelings of happiness, optimism, curiosity and connectedness, as well as decreased anxiety, depression, rumination and fear of failure. Self-compassion, according to Neff, means three things:

1. Be mindful of how you are feeling. It is essential to recognize your emotions.
2. Be kind to yourself.
3. Accept your human-ness.

When you go through difficulties, you might hear a voice inside your head that judges, criticizes, and shames you. This inner critic can take its toll on your emotions and self-worth. The inner critic serves a purpose in that it helps you recognize where you have gone wrong and what you might need to do to set things right. Often, what you might be missing is your inner nurturer that brings about self-compassion and encouragement.

The opposites of your inner critic are self-acceptance and self-compassion. When your inner critic beats you up for challenges, you can become upset, beaten down, and hopeless. It is common to blame or question yourself. The inner critic is sometimes called the critical inner voice. Everyone possesses an inner voice that can drag you down and make you feel worse. When you stand up to your inner critic and shift towards your inner nurturer, you will bring about more self-compassion and encouragement in the face of struggle.

There are two different voices inside your head: the critical one and the nurturing one. The critical voice can bring you down and weigh heavy on your mind. The voice that is encouraging brings self-compassion and encouragement. The good news is that you can choose which voice you want to listen to and give attention to. First, decide which voice will provide the power. This will help you build resilience which is extremely empowering.

In the book, *Self-Compassion: The Proven Power of Being Kind to Yourself*, self-compassion researcher Dr. Kristin Neff teaches us about the proven power of being kind to ourselves. Positive self-talk techniques allow us to accept setbacks as a natural part of the human experience. She says it's time to "stop beating yourself up and leave insecurity and self-doubt behind."

According to Dr. Kristin Neff, having compassion for oneself is no different from giving compassion to others. Think about what it feels like to experience compassion.

- First, to have compassion for others, you must notice their suffering.
- Second, compassion involves feeling moved by others' suffering so that your heart responds to their pain. Did you know that the word compassion means to suffer with?
- Third, compassion also means you offer understanding and kindness to others when they fail or make mistakes rather than judge them harshly.

Self-compassion involves acting the same way towards yourself when you are having a difficult time, fail, or notice something you don't like about yourself or your situation. Instead of ignoring your pain, you stop to tell yourself: This is difficult right now. Then ask yourself, How can I comfort and care for myself now?

When you love someone with an addiction, it is common to feel inadequacies, shame, embarrassment, pain, and a sense of failure as you try to rescue your loved one. It is prevalent to think things like, "Why am I so stupid?" or "How am I letting this happen?" Often you end up judging or criticizing yourself. Self-compassion is self-love, where you show kindness towards yourself. When you go through challenging struggles in life, the elements of self-compassion and self-love are vital. Self-compassion brings about empathy and offerings of kindness and understanding towards yourself. Self-love is a state of appreciation and a choice to be compassionate towards yourself at any moment.

Self-compassion means being kind and understanding of imperfection, perceived failures, and negative emotions. It is about the human condition and the reality that all of us will have struggles and challenges. Loving someone who is addicted is a harrowing and difficult thing to navigate. It is essential to be gentle with yourself as you confront and experience these painful experiences.

Self-compassion experts teach you how to limit self-criticism and offset its adverse effects while enabling you to achieve your highest potential and a more peaceful, fulfilled life.

REFLECTION QUESTIONS:

- Do you suffer more from excessive self-criticism or negative self-talk?
- How can you still feel good about yourself when loving someone with an addiction?
- How can you offer self-compassion when in turmoil, manipulation, and despair?
- How will self-compassion help you?

SELF-ESTEEM AND SELF-COMPASSION

Renowned self-compassion researcher Dr. Kristin Neff explains how self-esteem and self-compassion differ in many ways. She describes self-esteem as your sense of self-worth, perceived values, or how much you like yourself. Self-compassion, in contrast, is not based on self-evaluations. You deserve self-love and compassion regardless of what particular set of traits you possess, regardless of what is going on around you.

Self-compassion encourages you to acknowledge your flaws and limitations, allowing you to look at things from a more realistic and objective perspective. It is also essential to make the distinction that self-love is not narcissism. Self-love is about loving yourself regardless of social comparison, performance, achievement, or the need for validation. On the other hand, narcissism relies on social comparison and validation from others. A self-focused, honest, and authentic appreciation for yourself is an excellent way to look at self-love.

Consider the moments when you most often experience compassion in your life. Most people understand compassion primarily in terms of their relationships. Maybe you helped a close friend with marriage challenges or helped a daughter who was ashamed about her performance. Because these individuals are loved ones, you respond to their suffering with kindness. You listen attentively to their feelings, don't judge them, and assure them they're still good people even amidst these challenges. This behaviour is how you show compassion for others. Self-compassion is more challenging to give than offering compassion to others. It is harder to see areas of suffering in your own life.

BARRIERS TO SELF-COMPASSION

Let's explore typical barriers to self-compassion. It is often easy to extend compassion toward others, yet many struggle to extend it to themselves. Why is it difficult to be nice to yourself? Because of the messages we receive, responding to yourselves with kindness and care can sometimes feel strange, ridiculous, pointless or even bring up feelings of disgust and anger. For most people, barriers will get in the way of their self-compassion journey. To give yourself the best chance of building self-compassion, it is helpful to check if these common obstacles apply to you too.

Here are some typical barriers to self-compassion:

Self-compassion can be painful: Sometimes, it is common to distract yourself when facing challenges in your life. You might find it easier to numb or deflect real emotions. Self-compassion can force you to confront memories and events that you might find painful.

Having a misconception about self-compassion: There are misconceptions and beliefs about self-compassion where some people fear becoming lazy, self-indulgent, self-absorbed, undisciplined and out of control.

Worry about being judged: Self-compassion empha-sizes connection with others based on a shared experience of suffering and struggles that we all face. You need to be vulnerable. Putting yourself out there and admitting you are struggling can be scary.

You believe self-criticism motivates: "I am such an idiot, I can't believe I did that, I am so useless, I need to do better, I should be doing better, other people don't make such stupid mistakes. I am just not careful enough, I have never been careful enough, and now I am failing and getting what I deserve." Does this sort of critical self-talk sound familiar to you? Deep down, you may believe that self-criticism has benefits as it motivates you; help you get things done. It toughens you up. It pushes you to excel and makes you a better person.

Negative Beliefs about Self-Compassion: Some people fear becoming lazy, self-indulgent, self-absorbed, undisciplined and out of control if engaging in self-com-passion. Some may be concerned that they would achieve nothing, get nothing done, make mistakes, stagnate in life and never progress.

WHY IS SELF-COMPASSION IMPORTANT FOR REGAINING YOUR POWER?

Self-compassion fosters positive emotions. It is a way of being on your own team and cheering for yourself. Over the past decade, eminent psychologists such as Martin Seligman and Mihalyi Csikszentmihalyi have become increasingly interested in how positive emotions like love, joy, curiosity, and hope can help maximize health and well-being. Generally known as the "positive psychology" movement, it focuses on understanding the factors that lead to mental health rather than mental illness. It is about cultivating strengths rather than eliminating weaknesses. You will have challenges and struggles in life and will never be perfect. Self-compassion fosters positive emotions, strengths, and resilience, allowing you to embrace your power.

Self-compassion moves you from judgment to kindness. Don't beat yourself up. You need love and support right now. Self-compassion is essential because it moves you from self-judgement to a place of self-kindness, from feeling isolated to understanding common humanity. Self-compassion also allows you to honour personal experiences mindfully and lovingly. You cannot ignore your pain. But you can support yourself through tough times. Through self-compassion, you can quiet your inner critic, recognize your authentic emotions, treat yourself with kindness, and increase compassion in all your relationships.

Self-compassion breeds confidence. Do you run ragged, trying to do it all and pick up all the broken pieces? Or Do you lose sleep ruminating over possible mistakes, worrying, or questioning? In her book *Brave, Not Perfect*, Reshma Saujani helps you break free from the trap of perfection and rewire yourself for bravery. Bravery gives you the power to hear your voice, to leave behind what makes you unhappy, and go for what sparks joy in your soul. By being brave, not perfect, you can become the author of your most meaningful, boldest, and most joyful life. Life shrinks or expands in proportion to one's courage. Courage, therefore, is the key to living the life we desire for ourselves.

Self-compassion acknowledges that you are human and not perfect. Sometimes you may seek perfection and put the needs of others above your own. Trying to make others around you happy might neglect your own needs and emotions. It takes bravery to let the world see the real you and your struggle when you love someone with an addiction. Shame causes many people to suffer in silence and alone. It is common to hold shame, embarrassment, and disappointment inside. It takes courage to allow someone to see the real you because life is not perfect when you love someone with an addiction. The more comfortable you get with doing, saying, and being in your truth, the less you'll get caught up in what others might say and do. You will build your bravery muscle to be vulnerable. You must offer yourself compassion and honour your truth at this time. Being compassionately brave means showing up with flaws and knowing you are not perfect. It also means being strong enough to reach out to others for support.

Compassion supports us through setbacks and struggles. Instead of lying to yourself to feel good, you can feel the peace of accepting yourself just as you are. Rather than loathing yourself for failures or setbacks, you'll recognize that disappointments and imperfections are typical experiences everyone shares. To truly feel good about yourself, you don't need to artificially boost your self-esteem, try to achieve more, or distract yourself; instead, you can develop better feelings about yourself by increasing your self-compassion. By treating yourself with kindness and accepting yourself exactly as you are, you can create authentic inner peace and feel better about yourself despite anything happening around you. Even the most successful people in the world will experience setbacks and obstacles at some point. One of the elements of self-compassion is self-forgiveness and the ability to conquer rejection from yourself and others so that you can bounce back.

SELF-COMPASSION FOR HEALING AND EMPOWERMENT

Walk yourself through self-compassion and notice the empowering effect it might have on you. The first step to tapping into self-compassion's healing qualities is identifying areas of suffering in your life. You can identify the areas of suffering in your life by asking yourself specific questions.

REFLECTION QUESTIONS:

How do you respond to problems?

- Do you focus solely on the challenge at hand, or do you step back to give yourself some comfort?
- Do you try to create solutions to problems right away?
- What would it look like to provide yourself with comfort?
- What comfort are you needing?

SAVING YOU IS KILLING ME: LOVING SOMEONE WITH AN ADDICTION

REFLECTION QUESTIONS:

Do you tend to catastrophize about your problems?

- Do you make bad situations seem worse?
- Do you ruminate and stay focused on the issue?
- Do you worry about things that are out of your control?
- Do you question or blame yourself?

Are you able to connect with other people when you're struggling?

- Does hardship make you feel even more isolated?
- Can you call a close friend who will commiserate about personal difficulties?
- Do you let these feelings fester into personal blame and turmoil?
- Do you feel ashamed and embarrassed to share your struggle with others?
- Where can you connect with others who would offer non-judgmental compassion?
- What are your areas of most internal suffering?

Take some time to reflect. After identifying areas of your life that cause the most internal suffering, you're ready to apply self-compassion basics.

ESSENTIAL COMPONENTS OF SELF-COMPASSION

According to self-compassion researcher Dr. Kristin Neff, there are three essential components of self-compassion: self-kindness, common humanity, and mindfulness. Walk yourself through these fundamental components of self-compassion.

SELF-KINDNESS - Being kind to yourself.

Self-kindness is the cessation of negative self-talk. It means that you've made an intentional choice to stop judging yourself for your suffering. By stepping back from your judgmental impulses, you'll have the power to understand your shortcomings and learn from them rather than condemning them. During your next difficult moment or when life is supposed to go a certain way and doesn't, tell yourself, "I'm sorry you feel upset," or, "Embarrassment is difficult." You might even hold yourself in a loving embrace to feel a physical sense of comfort. When you show comfort to yourself, you're acknowledging your pain, but you're also playing the role of the caregiver.

REFLECTION QUESTION:

- What can you do to give yourself some friendly comfort?

COMMON HUMANITY - We're all in this together.

Your feelings of shame and inadequacy are widespread among those who love someone dealing with an addiction, so you don't have to assume that your challenging circumstance is somehow unique to you. You are not alone. Dealing with the pain that comes from loving someone with an addiction is not something you have to do alone. And, if people are not dealing with addiction in their family, it will be some other struggle or circumstance. Hurdles make you normal, not uniquely terrible. Everyone sometimes falls short, makes mistakes, and feels shame. When you experience a spouse's addiction relapse or your marriage disintegrates, you might assume these unwanted events prove that your life is all wrong. It doesn't mean you should see these challenges as proof of your inadequacy. Instead, figure out ways and why this makes you normal. It makes sense that you feel this way - this is hard! You are not alone in this.

REFLECTION QUESTIONS:

- How are you isolating yourself?
- Why does your challenge make you human?

MINDFULNESS - Being mindful of what is.

Mindfulness is a powerful tool that helps you observe your feelings and life events with calm and compassion. Mindfulness is essential because it can minimize your resistance attempts, such as avoiding shame, anxiety, and grief. For instance, during a moment of difficulty, you might feel the urge to jump into action to prevent your true feelings. You might go on a spending spree to distract yourself from your problems, throw yourself into a new project to forget about your miserable home life, or spend a lot of time at the bar to numb the grief. However, resistance ends up causing more harm than help, and fighting your emotions will only make them stronger. Observe these feelings and recognize them, non-judgmentally, for what they are. Mindfulness can be a space for practicing the habits of recognition and non-reactivity. Remember that self-awareness and non-reactivity are always available.

REFLECTION QUESTION:

- Without judgment, what are some feelings you are observing?

SELF-CRITICISM VS. SELF-COMPASSION

When you find yourself mentally being hard on yourself, it becomes crucial to stand up to your inner critic. It is too easy to get buried in a negative internal voice avalanche. Experiment with yourself by comparing self-criticism and self-compassion. One of the best ways to assess whether self-criticism helps and self-compassion hinders to compare the two. There are many benefits to self-compassion. However, you need to notice and decide what is best for you. Sometimes you believe being mean to yourself might motivate you to change. Science says that compassion is far more motivating than criticism. But it would help if you decided this for yourself. Since you might believe self-criticism is helpful and self-compassion is unhelpful to you, you need to compare what happens when you criticize yourself with what happens when you are kind towards yourself.

In this experiment, alternate between two days, being kind towards yourself on one day, then self-critical the next day. It could look something like this:

Kind-Day: On the first day, put all that usual self-criticism to the side as best you can, saving it up for the following day, and speak to yourself like you would someone you cared about. This kind-day is not about being unrealistically positive (e.g., "everything will be great") or heaping yourself with praise (e.g., "I am awesome"), but instead being encouraging and kind in your words and tone of voice.

Plan the Kind Day: Be clear about what sorts of things you will say to yourself and your tone of voice on your Kind Day (e.g., I will say something like "I know this is hard, everyone struggles with this, just do the best you can and hang in there," and I will have a soft, warm tone to my voice). What will you do when you catch yourself being critical?

Critical Day: On the second day, purposely be as critical towards yourself as possible. Berate and be harsh with yourself over every little thing, every mistake, everything you don't like about yourself and your efforts never being up to perfection.

Plan the Critical Day: Be clear about what sorts of things you will say to yourself and your tone of voice on your Critical Day (e.g., I will call myself an "idiot" a lot, say that "nothing I do is good enough, and I should do better" and be very cold and hard in my tone of voice to myself). Please note that if this type of day already seems uncomfortable to plan, you can skip the critical day.

Prediction 1: What do you think will happen on the days you are critical of yourself?

Prediction 2: What do you think will happen on the days you are kind to yourself?

REFLECTION QUESTIONS:

- What frequently happens on Kind Days?
- What frequently happens on Critical Days?
- How do the two different days support or hinder you?

If you found poorer outcomes on the days you criticized yourself compared to the days you were kind; then hopefully, this enhances your motivation to put all your efforts into building self-compassion. If you find no difference in outcomes between the two days, you won't lose anything by trying a new kinder way of treating yourself. If you found better outcomes on the days you were critical compared to the days you were kind to yourself; researchers would question whether you were being kind to yourself. Now that you have challenged and experimented with your positive beliefs about self-criticism and negative beliefs about self-compassion. What are your conclusion and findings?

Challenge When You Think Self-Criticism Is Helpful

Below is a list of questions you can ask yourself to challenge whether your positive beliefs about self-criticism are really true. You can use this evidence for and evidence against the formula for any belief you'd like to dispute in the future.

Evidence For

What makes you think self-criticism is helpful?

What is the evidence for your positive beliefs?

Can you specifically describe how self-criticism helps?

Is the evidence for your beliefs good/solid/reliable?

How could the evidence for your beliefs be viewed?

Evidence Against

Is there any evidence that goes against your positive beliefs about self-criticism?

What is the goal of your self-criticism?

Does self-criticism achieve this goal?

Can you achieve your goals without self-criticism? (i.e., instead of encouraging yourself or taking action)

Is self-criticism helpful or something else? (i.e., motivating? spurs you to take action)

What are the negative consequences of being self-critical?

How is self-criticism damaging to you?

If being critical is so helpful, would you use it to deal with a friend or child struggling with something? If not, why not?

Have you ever conducted a proper experiment, comparing the outcome of being critical versus kind to yourself?

If you haven't done this, how do you genuinely know that self-criticism is helping you?

STAND UP TO THE INNER CRITIC

In his book *Resilient: How to Grow An Unshakeable Core of Calm*, Strength, and Happiness, psychologist Rick Hanson offers some advice on how to stand up to your inner critic:

First Step: Observe The Inner Critic

1. Try to observe and listen to the self-criticism that is going on inside your head already.

2. Take notice of repetitive thoughts that feel and are discouraging.

3. Pay close attention to any hostile or angry expressions towards yourself. The inner critic can be harsh, completely rude, and absurd.

4. Look at your inner critic as something that lacks credibility and truth. You can even give your inner critic a name like Mean Mary or Crusty Kim.

Second Step: Add the Caring Committee

When the inner critic comes to play, turn to your inner nurturer to protect yourself. The inner nurturer is encouraging and loving, especially when things are stressful, disappointing, or terrible. Rick Hansen calls this contrasting voice (the inner nurturer) the caring committee.

REFLECTION QUESTIONS:

- Who's on your caring committee?
- What would you name it?

Third Step: Talk Back to Your Inner Critic

Argue against what the inner critic is saying. Paying attention, catching your inner critic's claims, and writing them down can make you see how ridiculous the inner critic might be. Then ask members of the caring committee to step in. Consider how others value you and see you as a good person worthy of love and care. Turn up the volume of the inner nurturer. You might talk back to your inner critic and say, *That's not true because* _____. You can repeat the statement over and over with different answers. Or you could make statements to the inner critic like *Another way of seeing this is* _____. Repeat over and over until you don't have any more answers.

Fourth Step: Power Up Your Self-Talk

Words that you tell yourself become your life and reality for you. Self-talk is simply the act of talking to yourself either out loud or mentally inside your head. It can be nurturing or critical. The messages that you tell yourself will encourage and motivate you, or they have the potential to limit, upset, and even hold you back. Be grateful and start talking to yourself like a best friend or a caring parent. Use positive words and vocabulary whenever you can to get yourself out of a negative inner critic rut. Replace negative critical thoughts with positive nurturing ones. Try using positive affirmations, mantras, or postings all over your space to help you encourage your inner nurturer.

REFLECTION QUESTION:

- How will you power up your self-talk?

INNER CRITIC AWARENESS

Understanding the origin of the inner critic will help you not take your thoughts personally or too seriously. The brain thinks about 60-70 thousand thoughts a day. Take a step back with self-awareness and look at this whole slide-show of thoughts without being entangled in them. You can distance yourself from the impact of thoughts and not take them as a voice of truth. The inner critic has value since it is trying to keep you safe. In a way, it is merely doing its job, trying to protect you from future hurt, embarrassment, or rejection. The problem is that it does not go away and plays like a broken record, continually repeating itself. It would be best to acknowledge the inner critic's value while intercepting it when it is not helpful or relevant. It becomes a balancing act.

Since humans are social creatures, your need for love and affection is paramount, and the critic is trying to help us keep harmony. Humans need to be loved and feel like someone cares for them. The critic is there to help you survive and avoid humiliation or loss of love. The problem with the mechanism is that the critic does not know how or where to stop. It is also common to create a mistaken loyalty to the critic. The inner critic does an excellent job of attacking your sense of self-worth. In the book *Make Peace with Your Mind*, Mark Coleman teaches how mindfulness and compassion can free you from your inner critic. Coleman offers some of the following tips to help you work with your inner critic:

RECOGNIZING THE INNER CRITIC:

STEP 1: Use mindful awareness to recognize when it is operating. Notice that voice.

STEP 2: Start to pay attention when those thoughts are coming up. Notice what they are saying. Say: "hello judgments," and recognize that they are thoughts, not the truth. You can even give your inner critic a name. "There is Mean Mary again." "Crusty Kim is coming out to tear me down." "Annoying Alison is making an appearance."

STEP 3: Question the thoughts themselves. Thoughts are not always accurate. Consider where that thought might have come from and whose critical voice it might be.

STEP 4: Begin to remember your gifts, experiences, and talents, which stand in direct opposition to the self-doubting thoughts. See the funny side of the critic and even talk back to it. Question the view of the inner critic.

STEP 5: Replace judgment with discernment. Think about something problematic in your life that needs attention. Notice if any of your decisions are negative towards yourself. "Stupid me keeps putting up with this crap; you'd think I'd learn." Do your judgments imply you are wrong or less worthy? How do the judgments make you feel? Move to a place of discernment with no judgment. View the same things from a place of learning, growing, and managing. "It makes sense that I stay as long as I am; I love this man. This is challenging." Can you see the difference between approaching a situation with judgment and viewing it with discernment? Defend yourself against judgments.

STEP 6: Befriend yourself. Turn from self-hatred to self-kindness. Move from self-harm to self-compassion and from self-blame to self-forgiveness, giving up hope of a better past. In other words, you can't change the past once it is over.

PROCESSING SETBACKS: THE COMPASSIONATE WAY

Setbacks are a part of life. Setbacks can be problematic. Be gentle with your heart as you heal and recover. Since it is a part of life to have a plot twist, how do you compassionately navigate setbacks? Here are some strategies you can use to become more resilient, optimistic, and able to bounce back after or during setbacks:

1. Accept what is happening with no judgment.
2. Honour and sit with your feelings.
3. Accept the part that you are responsible for.
4. Learn from your mistakes and spot the growth opportunity.
5. Don't dwell, blame, or listen to the inner critic.
6. Forgive yourself and offer self-compassion.
7. Find a way to be grateful. Even when things are terrible.

Inspirations to process setbacks with self-compassion:

Don't Beat Yourself Up: When you love someone with an addiction, you are already going through so much turmoil. The last thing you want to do is beat yourself up. It's essential to forgive yourself, let go of any pain you are holding onto, and accept that you are still a good person even amidst this relationship. You might get upset about the type of person you choose to be with or think you're the worst parent, and you might even get mad at yourself for not seeing red flags or for tolerating things you would never typically endure. There are many challenges to navigate when it comes to someone else's addiction. Essentially, you might be beating yourself up, thinking, "Why did I let this person take advantage of me?" or, "What was I thinking?" When you forgive yourself, you do not pretend things never happened, but quite the contrary. Forgiving yourself is about acknowledging your emotions and thoughts and being okay with what is coming up for you.

Practice Acceptance: Accept yourself, your emotions, and even your flaws. You are not "less" of a person because of what you are going through. Surrender to the pain you are experiencing, and be patient with yourself. Do a best friend test. Imagine your best friend is telling you about the same situation you are going through: How would you support them? What would you tell them? What advice would you give? Be kind to yourself and cheer for your suffering to end, just like a best friend or beloved family member would do.

Remember You're a Good Person: Remember that you are not wrong or bad just because you find yourself in a challenging time. You can do something wrong, make a bad decision, or date someone with an addiction, but this does not make you a bad person. Mistakes, failures, and disappointments are a part of being human and a part of your growth. Be patient and kind with yourself as a way back to clarity. It is common to get pulled into the muck when you love someone with an addiction. Remember, you are doing your best and trying your best to navigate this heart-wrenching circumstance. You are a good person! Acknowledge that you are worthy of peace, stability, and a happy life.

Talk to People: Talking to someone else about challenges and what bothers you can have many benefits. You will gain another perspective as you work through emotions and different views. Other people are less critical of you and will offer compassion and encouragement. Reach out to a friend, family member, or professional. Time, space and compassion are some of the best ways to heal. Friendships and support groups will help you lovingly process the pain and inner conflict. Reaching out is a way to understand you are not alone and that others are going through the same difficulties.

Treat Yourself Well: Take good care of yourself and try to do things like
- Meditate.
- Spend time in nature.

- Pamper yourself.
- Be present in the moment.
- Take care of your needs.
- Express your passion.
- Be grateful for yourself.

For more ideas, there is an entire chapter in this book on self-care!

Know You Are Not Alone: Tap into the loving power of human connections. Social connection is more important than you think when facing challenges and struggles. Social connections can lower anxiety and depression, regulate emotions, and increase self-esteem. Human connection and shared humanity are a part of self-compassion. Social connections can improve your psychological well-being and physical health. Studies have shown that a lack of social connections is a more significant detriment to our health than obesity or smoking. Science has shown that people who feel more connected to others have lower rates of anxiety and depression.

Brené Brown, professor at the University of Houston Graduate College of Social Work, emphasizes that we all share the need for a deep sense of love and belonging. She explains that we are social creatures and are biologically, cognitively, physically, and spiritually wired to love, be loved, and belong. It is common and normal to feel alone or lonely when you struggle, like loving someone with an addiction. There is shame, embarrassment, and concern involved that can be hard to share. You can rarely lean on the addicted loved one struggling with addiction. Even when they are present, sometimes they have become empty vessels of humans and completely different people preoccupied with their addiction.

As Dr. Chris Peterson, one of the founding fathers of Positive Psychology, would lovingly put it: "Other People Matter." In the "Other People Matter" mindset, there are five elements intended to help people understand ways to build positive relationships in their own lives as well as the elements each of us needs in our lives:

- Identifying and appreciating the good in ourselves and others.
- Knowing words and actions affects ourselves and others.
- Supporting others when they struggle as well as ourselves.
- Cheering others' successes as well as our own.
- Being present and giving others and ourselves attention.

Friends can help you deal with stress, make healthy lifestyle choices that foster strength, and allow you to bounce back from challenges more quickly. Social connections are essential for mental health. Spending time with positive friends, colleagues, or family can improve your outlook. Society can be very isolated when dealing with someone with an addiction. You may feel very alone. Fostering friendships and human connection helps to make your life more balanced, complete, and fun.

There are many benefits to reaching out to others. Friends and other people can; offer encouragement and support, boost your self-esteem, be a powerful positive influence, increase your sense of belonging and purpose, provide a happiness boost and reduction of stress, and support to help you cope with trauma.

When you feel alone, remember that other people feel the same. You are not meant to "do life" alone. There are so many people struggling alongside you in a similar place. We all need to help each other and keep moving forward. Even if you don't have a friend to talk to, many others have endured a similar struggle. My message here to you is to **reach out!** I created the Facebook online community, meetings, podcast and this book to support you. If you still need to reach out to us, please do. You are never alone. www.savingyouiskillingme.com

REFLECTION QUESTIONS:

- Who can you talk to?
- Who can you lean on?
- What family member can you call?
- What group can you join?

You will be amazed if you open up and ask for help at the amount of support available to you. I am always here for you too. Just go to my website and set up a call with me!

In a world where you might feel like you're going crazy, a friend can offer a new lens through which to see the world. Having someone to talk to helps to process feelings and work through possible solutions. Social connections allow for shared experiences and personal growth. Support from a professional or loved one can show you the right direction and sometimes open your eyes to new ideas, something you might be missing, or a different approach you can take. Social connections are those people who can wipe your tears when you cry, support you when you feel broken, offer a shoulder to cry on, and encourage you when you are down. The most important thing is for you to realize you are not alone.

SEND YOURSELF SOME LOVE

Write yourself a love letter. I know it sounds crazy, but writing yourself a love letter is a beautiful way to practice self-compassion during tough times. Writing a letter to yourself gives you a new perspective and teaches you some valuable lessons. It is common to express love to others, but you rarely take the opportunity for self-reflection and self-compassion. The crucial part of this exercise is to write a letter in the third person, which would sound like Dear _____ (your name). I love how you _____. As you write a love letter to yourself, ensure you cultivate gratitude and appreciation. You can ask yourself some questions. You might talk about what lessons you have learned and what precious knowledge you gain from this experience. You can share your beliefs. You could pretend that this letter is your future self writing to your current self. In this letter, you can thank and give yourself honour and appreciation. You might thank yourself for being strong, asking for support, helping others, or tapping into resources you didn't know you had. You might journal or place your letter on paper with a special letterhead.

Start this letter to yourself by answering the following prompts:

I love how _____.

I love how you're passionate about _____.

I am proud of you for _____.

I know you feel loved when _____.

I love that you are learning _____.

I love how powerful you _____.

I love how you handled _____.

I am so sorry you _____.

What I admire most about you is _____.

Feel free to put this letter somewhere special and read it whenever you need a boost. Don't be surprised if tears of love well up in your eyes. You know you are lovable and valuable to this world. Sometimes a reminder is needed. Some of my clients send a letter to their mailboxes.

30-DAY SELF-COMPASSION CHALLENGE.

In the next 30 days, how can you show yourself compassion and self-love? Can you make a plan for self-compassion? What can you do for the next 30 days that will demonstrate self-love and self-compassion? Write it out and adhere to your self-compassion challenge for 30 days.

For the next 30 days, I will _____.

You build your ability to cope by giving yourself support and encouragement rather than being cold and judgmental when challenges and difficulties arise. Turning towards understanding, acceptance, and inward love can help you regain your power when suffering, hurting, or feeling knocked down. Self-compassion is one of the most powerful gifts you can give yourself to help you cope and build resilience.

KEY TAKE-AWAYS

- ⊘ Self-compassion means three things: Being mindful of how you are feeling. It is essential to recognize your emotions. You are being kind to yourself and accepting your human-ness.

- ✓ Self-compassion encourages you to acknowledge your flaws and limitations, allowing you to look at things from a more realistic and objective perspective. Self-esteem differs from self-compassion in that self-esteem is your sense of self-worth, perceived values, or how much you like yourself.

- ✓ Three essential components of self-compassion are self-kindness, common humanity, and mindfulness.

- ✓ Self-compassion is more potent and motivating than self-criticism and contributes to your well-being.

- ✓ Replace negative critical thoughts with positive nurturing ones. You have more than one voice inside your head. Speak to the inner critic with the inner nurturer.

- ✓ Setbacks are a part of life. Setbacks can be discouraging. Be gentle with your heart as you heal and recover by processing setbacks with self-compassion.

CHAPTER REFLECTION QUESTIONS:

Take a moment to write down your highlights from this chapter:

- What takeaways are going to inspire you the most going forward?

- What brought a significant or slight shift in your thinking, feelings, or behaviour?

CHAPTER FIVE

You Can Say No: Set Healthy Boundaries and Boost Your Self-Respect

"Daring to set boundaries is about having the courage to love ourselves even when we risk disappointing others."
— *Brene Brown.*

Self-Respect is often a neglected but essential concept. Sometimes you might forget that you are worthy of the proper respect or treatment as a human being. Tapping back into your standards and personal values to set appropriate boundaries or limits is crucial. If setting boundaries seems overwhelming, you're not alone. Learn how to set boundaries with a loved one struggling with addiction to save your self-respect. Boundaries are essential in any relationship, but they're even more important when a friend or loved one has an addiction.

A partner struggling with addiction can seem like a completely different person, and you might feel lost, exhausted, frustrated, and afraid for your safety. In this section, you will understand what self-respect is and why it is essential to regain your power while learning how to set boundaries, meet your needs, and deal with difficult people. Boundaries and self-respect are vital to creating healthy relationships, even when your loved one isn't healthy.

In this chapter, you will discover the following:
- What is self-respect, and why it's crucial to your well-being.
- What are codependency and enabling, and how it relates to self-respect?
- What narcissism is and how it relates to addiction.
- What gaslighting is and how to guard yourself.
- How to set boundaries and safeguard your well-being.

WHAT IS SELF-RESPECT?

Self-respect is holding yourself in esteem and believing you are worthy of being treated well. Having self-respect in a relationship means you hold yourself to your standards and are not pushed beyond these boundaries. When you love someone with an addiction or are in a relationship with someone who has an addiction, chances are your limits have been pushed, and your boundaries are blurred. You may not feel like you have much self-respect. Luckily, self-respect isn't static. You can cultivate, change, and grow from it. It's always possible to establish boundaries. Self-respect starts with you.

When someone you love has an addiction, getting stuck on their emotional rollercoaster is prevalent. You might feel unsafe at times. Self-respect is about setting healthy boundaries, and it is even more important when you care about someone with an addiction. Since you are all responsible for your actions in your own lives, you determine what type of behaviour you allow others to display towards you.

Self-respect is about acknowledging that it's essential not to take on the consequences of another person's addiction as your own. Boundaries are rules or guidelines that you can establish to protect your well-being. It's almost like drawing a line in the sand to ensure you are not taken advantage of or treated unacceptably. Self-respect involves thinking about what you will allow in your life and what you won't put up with any longer. It consists of thinking about the behaviour that others exhibit that harms your well-being. Claiming your boundaries and practicing self-respect isn't always easy, and you can feel uncomfortable. Setting boundaries becomes essential for your mental health and emotional well-being.

One of the most important things to know and realize is that no boundary you set will solve someone's addiction. Putting boundaries in place is for you and your self-respect.

Building self-respect has to be done consistently over some time. Practicing self-respect is essential to regain your power. An example of self-respect is asserting yourself in relationships to get the treatment you deserve to feel proud and optimistic. How you take care of yourself is critical to your quality of life. Self-respect comes from how you view yourself and what you think you deserve.

The good news is that there are things that you can do to increase your self-respect. Self-respect is a form of self-love wherein you value your own unique space in this world. Self-respect is more than just affirming yourself; it is also a belief in yourself and the fact that you are worthy of love, attention, and respect and that you are no less than anyone else. Self-respect is the knowledge that you are respected and expect to be treated well and respectfully. Having self-respect helps others to see and treat you with dignity and worth.

BUILDING SELF-RESPECT

Remembering what you value and what's important to you: Self-respect is about knowing you are worthy and treating yourself accordingly. One of my favourite ways to help my clients tap into and reestablish their self-respect is to help them remember what they value and what is important to them. Self-respect is about honouring what you value and love and ensuring they exist in your life. I appreciate beauty, so I make sure that I surround myself with beautiful things in my environment, keep a tidy home, and I get out into nature as often as possible. I don't feel good when the kids make a disaster in the house, and I don't get outside. My need for beauty still needs to be met. You can see how from there, it is easy to make a boundary with my children and my schedule.

Self-respect has a lot to do with honouring and acting by your values. Remembering what you value will give you clues as to what is essential to you. When you get clear on what you love and hold these values in high regard for your life, you can better regain your power. When you are reacquainted with what matters most, it becomes easier to be clear on what you do and don't desire for your life. For example, if you value simplicity, keeping things simple and not complex in your life is essential. When things get complicated, you might be triggered and feel uncomfortable. Self-awareness of what you value is an excellent place to start building self-respect.

Values Assessment: Take a look at a big list of possible values or use the mini list of values below and circle which values resonate as important to you. Some examples of values are:

Abundance, Availability, Balance, Beauty, Bravery, Carefulness, Closeness, Comfort, Commitment, Delight, Dependability, Energy, Enjoyment, Entertainment, Fairness, Faith, Fame, Growth, Guidance, Happiness, Honesty, Honor, Hopefulness, Intimacy, Kindness, Knowledge, Leadership, Looking good, Love, Mindfulness, Modesty, Open-mindedness, Openness, Optimism, Passion, Peace, Perceptiveness, Playfulness, Pleasantness, Pleasure, Recreation, Refinement, Reflection, Relaxation, Self-control, Selflessness, Self-reliance, Stillness, Strength, Structure, Thankfulness, Thoroughness, Thoughtfulness, Virtue, Vision, Vitality, Wonder, Youthfulness, Zeal.

Use this list as inspiration. Narrow down your list to the top 5-10 things you value.

REFLECTION QUESTIONS:

- What do you value most in life?
- What is important to you in your life?
- Are your daily actions taking you closer or further away from the things you value most?

Identify and nurture your needs: If self-respect is about taking care of yourself and honouring what you value, you must identify what "care" means. Consider:

- What do you value?
- What is important to you?
- What are your needs?
- What would make you feel fulfilled and satisfied?

Use your values and what is important to you as a clue into what your needs are. If you value trust, for example, what would you need? You probably need reliability, consistency, and faithfulness in a partner or friends.

Check-in with your needs daily, and instead of shaming yourself for having needs, nurture your needs. Attending to your needs is essential to your well-being and a form of self-respect. Ask yourself the following.

What am I needing? What am I feeling? What am I wanting? Keep in mind as you connect to your needs that you only have control over yourself and your behaviour.

REFLECTION QUESTIONS:

- What do you need for yourself?
- What do you want for yourself?

A NO-SHAME PERSPECTIVE ON CODEPENDENCY AND ENABLING?

It's important to note here that there is no shame in the fact that you might have let your guard down and let your level of self-respect drop as a result. When you love some-one with an addiction, it is a very different circumstance and losing connection to your values and needs can hap-pen slowly over time. Codependency and enabling are common concepts you will hear when involved in the recovery world. Let me explain them from a loving and compassionate perspective toward you.

As a healthy, loving, and kind person, you only want the best for the struggling person you love. You do everything you can to help and support your loved one. The only problem is that this can worsen the addiction and destroy you. When your loved one has an addiction, all the typical things you would do to offer your suffering loved one support go out the window. You are a good person and human.

You are doing your best, given this challenging situation.

Enabling refers to the positive act of helping someone accomplish something that they could not do alone. Enabling also refers to helping someone in such a way that rather than solving a problem is making a situation worse. You may unknowingly be enabling the addict because you think you are helping those you love.

Codependency is a theory that attempts to explain imbalanced relationships where one person enables another person's self-destructive behaviour. Codependency often has you funnelling your energy into supporting the people in your life without making space for, or even considering, what you need for yourself. The signs of codependency typically include putting your needs on the back burner to prioritize somebody else's needs.

My boyfriend, who hid his addiction from me for years, led me to believe he was suffering from a chronic sinus infection and depression. I tried to be supportive of his life as much as humanly possible. He was sleeping all day, so he couldn't work. I paid for his truck and all the bills while I caught him stealing from my wallet. I even remember getting him special supplements, essential oils, and vaporizers for his "stuffed nose." He would stay up all night, unable to sleep, so I got him magnesium to help him. Ironically, nothing worked. I fell into the codependency trap of trying to be a loving and supportive partner. He relied on me, and I continued to drop my needs to support his needs. We became co-dependent.

I became concerned, consumed, and completely worried about him. He was not right, and I lost the lovely man I fell madly in love with to drugs. I would get glimmers of love and special promises, only to be let down repeatedly. He would have terrible mood swings, and I would excuse his behaviour as I thought he was depressed and struggling. I let bizarre, terrible, manipulating, and hostile behaviour go on even though I knew in my heart this was wrong. But still, I let my self-respect and boundaries fall by the wayside. I did what anyone would do when they loved someone who was suffering. I became an enabler while believing I was being a loving, supportive partner.

Codependency and enabling are harsh words to hear when entangled in a painful, toxic mess of a relationship with an addict. I like to think I am a strong individual, and I bet you are as well, but addiction is a different situation. I fell into the trap of being an enabler and exhibiting codependent behaviours without realizing it. You might be as well. It is prevalent and incredibly human to become codependent and an enabler when you are in a relationship with an addicted loved one.

Loving and Caring Humans Become Codependent and Enable:

Why do so many well-meaning family members or spouses of someone with an addiction unintentionally enable the behaviours of their addicted loved one? When addiction is present, the addict's only desire is to be comfortable while continuing to use. We, the loved ones, knowingly or unknowingly want to fulfil their needs to support the person we love. It makes perfect sense when examining the situation.

What ends up happening, though, is the person with the addiction gets comfortable in their addiction, and you get comfortable or trained in supporting your loved one. The word codependency comes from the idea that two people become dependent on each other. All too often, the loved one with addiction usually depends on the family or spouse to provide financial support as they become less and less capable of caring for their own needs. They also rely on the family or spouse to give the love they cannot provide or feel for themselves.

When you love someone with an addiction, you usually also need to feel like a good spouse, girlfriend, boyfriend, parent, child, sibling, or friend. The addicted loved ones know this, and they can manipulate and take advantage of the people closest to them and get away with it. In the book *Love Smacked*, Sherry Gaba identifies the typical codependency patterns in toxic relationships and the adverse effects of codependency. She explains that sometimes you can get addicted to a relationship and love that you stay in a relationship longer than is healthy or bounce to another without allowing yourself time to heal. Even if it's inconsistent, unhealthy and unstable, connection and love become the top priority. You might tolerate more than you should, stay longer than is healthy and lose touch with your needs.

RECOGNIZING CODEPENDENCY

Without any shame or judgment, see if any of these statements resonate with you:

- You feel responsible for others.
- You worry about others' feelings, thoughts, actions, and choices.
- You feel anxiety and stress when someone else has a problem.
- You feel frustrated and disappointed when your help isn't practical.
- You tend to anticipate what others need and try to meet their needs.
- You become preoccupied with someone else's needs instead of your own.
- You find yourself flexing your boundaries.
- You find yourself saying yes when you mean no. You end up doing things you don't want to do or allow.
- You feel guilty when you say no or create boundaries.
- You abandon your routine to help others.
- Your world gets pulled into someone else's world.
- Another's problems become your own.

When you are codependent and putting someone else's needs above your own, it is typical for your self-respect, boundaries and needs to be sacrificed. This book is all about regaining your power and focusing back on yourself. Don't change the loving, caring, kind person that you are. Boundary tools are coming! Since reading this book, you are already starting to see the benefits of prioritizing your well-being and safeguarding your mental health.

REFLECTION QUESTIONS:

- What aspect of codependency surprised you?
- How has being a loving, kind person made you more likely to be codependent and an enabler?

WHAT IS NARCISSISM?

One of the most complex parts of loving someone with an addiction is that their behaviour is unpredictable and not typical. A tendency towards narcissism is present in everyone, to a degree. Narcissism is when someone has an inflated sense of importance and lacks empathy for others. Narcissism and addiction go hand and hand.

A blend of narcissism and addictive behaviour is overpowering, relentless, and abusive. But deep down, is every addict also a narcissist? And is every narcissist an addict? In his book, The Narcissist You Know, Joseph Burgo includes the "Addicted Narcissist" as one type of narcissism. While all addicts aren't narcissists, there are commonalities. Addicts and narcissistic personalities have many common features, including a pronounced lack of empathy for the people around them. They also focus selfishly on their addiction at the expense of the people around them. Burgo also mentions that a deep-rooted sense of shame is at the core of narcissism and addictive behaviours.

The destructive blend of selfishness and the belief that they do not have a problem leads to devastating consequences. There is debate about what comes first; narcissism? Or does addiction bring on narcissistic-like behaviours? Regardless, narcissistic traits tend to be present in people with an addiction. They may or may not have the personality disorder, but they tend to become self-absorbed, entitled, exploitative, and aggressive. They tend to be apathetic or lacking in empathy and put themselves first. Essentially, loving and respecting others is not balanced with self-importance, and they prioritize their needs and desires.

A person who is a narcissist or has an addiction tends to

- Lack empathy.
- Have high self-importance.
- Have a false image projection (they won't admit they have a problem), break the rules and think they are above 'normal' people.
- Turn on the charm when it suits them.
- Manipulate people's thoughts and emotions to suit their needs.
- Blame others when things aren't going as planned.

When you are in a relationship with someone who struggles with addiction and narcissism, you may find it extremely difficult and confusing about what you should be doing, saying, thinking, and feeling. The first step is understanding addiction and narcissism to gain footing and establish self-protection and the need for boundaries. Addiction tends to progress because many, like my boyfriend, are very good at hiding their behaviour. If you were to treat addiction like an illness or disease, you tend to offer empathy, concern, and support. However, addiction and narcissistic tendencies require a very different response. Empathy, support, and concern are not helpful in many cases.

Addiction is very confusing; many professionals in the recovery world believe addiction is a disease. It may start with a choice, but it does change the brain and becomes a disease. Still, it is a disease like no other. It can be a messy disease that brings manipulation, stealing, lying, and abusive behaviours. In other words, you will not likely tend to your addicted loved one like a loved one with cancer or any other disease.

Dealing With Addiction and Narcissism

Craig Malkin, a therapist and the author of *Rethinking Narcissism* discusses dealing with someone with addiction and narcissism issues. Although addiction makes the addicted loved one more narcissistic (willing to lie, steal, cheat, and even exploit others to feed their addiction), it is essential to understand that narcissism is a legitimate mental health condition that requires diagnosis by a mental health professional. Still, people with an addiction can exhibit narcissistic characteristics without having the disorder. Regardless, here are some practical ways to deal with someone with these tendencies.

See the reality of the situation: The addict in your life can get good at turning on a façade. Pretending everything is okay, making empty promises, and convincing you and others that everything is okay. Before you get drawn in, please pay attention when you catch them lying, manipulating, or outright disrespecting you. Despite what the addict in your life might say to you, your needs and wants are likely unimportant to them. The first step here is to see things as they are without making excuses or getting manipulated.

Shift the focus off of the addict and onto you: This step is about breaking the spell they have on you. Attention seems to gravitate toward the addicted loved one in your life. Whether it's negative or positive attention, narcissistic addicts tend to work hard to put themselves first and push your needs aside. To gain back your self-respect, don't allow them to infiltrate your sense of strength, self, and desires. Shift the focus back onto yourself. Take care of yourself first and remind yourself that it's not your job to fix them.

Speak up for yourself: When you love someone with an addiction, there are so many challenges. It becomes crucial to pick your battles. Addicts tend to enjoy picking fights and making others tense. It can give them a "reason" to go and feed their addiction. The best response is not to get flustered or overly annoyed, as this will only feed them to continue. You can express how their words and actions impact your life. Communicate what is not acceptable and how you expect to be treated. Often, they will not care or even understand.

Set clear boundaries: The addicted loved one in your life is often self-absorbed. They tend to cross many boundaries and not even see that they are doing so. Sometimes even the consequences of crossing boundaries won't matter to them. That is why you must be very clear about your boundaries and why they are essential. The addicted loved one in your life may only start paying attention to the boundaries you set that will affect them personally. Boundaries are not threats. (More on boundary setting in the next section.)

Expect disappointment: When you stand up for yourself and decide to practice self-respect, you can expect the addicted loved one in your life to be disappointed. When you speak up and set boundaries, someone may make you feel guilty or believe that what you ask is unreasonable or even controlling. Expect disappointment when you are claiming your self-respect. Be ready to stand your ground.

Remember you are not at fault: What comes with addiction is often blame. The addicted loved one in your life will seldom take responsibility for bad decisions or for hurting you. Remember that none of this is your fault. You did not cause this addiction to happen, nor have you influenced it in any way. Blame is a manipulation tool. No matter what they say or do, remember you are not at fault.

Reach out and connect with others: Connect with others that offer you a healthy relationship and support system. Try to spend less and less time in a relationship that feels toxic and challenging. Addiction and the narcissism that comes with it can be excruciatingly exhausting, leaving you drained. Connect with family, friends, and support groups. Get out into your community and find ways to reconnect with people.

Insist on the action, not promises: Addicted loved ones are good at making promises they cannot keep. They promise you what they know you want to hear and that they will do better. They also seem very sincere with all of their promises. You may even get a love letter! The bottom line is actions speak louder than words. They use promises as a form of manipulation to get what they need. Pay attention to their actions and see if they match their words, more on this in the next section.

Seek out help and acknowledge they need help: All too often, people with an addiction don't see a problem with themselves. As a result, they don't usually seek help or desire change. It is important to remember that you cannot cure them of their addiction. They have to want to get help. You can make suggestions to help, but you cannot make them do it. Focus on yourself and recognize when you need help. Dealing with someone with an addiction can affect your mental and physical health. Reach out for help.

Know when to move on: This is one of the most challenging realizations you can face when you love someone with an addiction. You wish for the person you loved, which is no longer present, to come back to you; this hope alone can keep you stuck. No one wants to abandon the suffering person. It becomes hard to acknowledge when you must move on, whether leaving an addicted spouse, stepping back from a loved one, or moving on.

Love from a distance: You can always love from a distance. When you experience threats, accusations, name-calling, blaming, isolation, manipulation, lying, cheating, humiliation, or verbal or emotional abuse, it's generally best to leave the relationship or love from a distance. Some tough questions to ask yourself are: Why am I here? Why do I continue to stay? What do I need to do?

Discarding is a typical behaviour: Narcissistic discard is when a person with an addiction and narcissistic tendencies ends their relationship with you. It can often feel like you've been used and discarded. The addicted narcissist sees people as objects they use to meet their needs and discard when the person no longer serves a purpose for them. If you get in the way of their addiction, discarding is typical. An addict will discard when people can no longer get boosted or be the fuel to replenish their addiction. If a narcissist addict has discarded you, you probably feel hurt and rejected. Give yourself time to heal, tap into your self-worth, focus on yourself, reach out for support, practice self-care, rebuild your life, update your boundaries, absorb all the learning, cut ties or love from a distance, and keep moving forward. And keep reading this book!

GASLIGHTING: THE TOOL OF MANIPULATION

Gaslighting is a common manipulation tool among those with an addiction. When you love someone with an addiction, you may find their behaviour confusing and upsetting. Common to all addictions are lying and manipulation. When manipulation confuses your reality, it is hard to stay calm and centred, nothing seems to make sense, and validity is challenged. Addiction-induced narcissism is common, and gaslighting is a typical tool of manipulation they use. Facts and truth are distorted, and knowing what to believe and how to stay balanced in manipulation becomes challenging. Arming yourself with knowledge becomes key to preserving your self-respect.

According to the Google dictionary, gaslighting is a form of psychological manipulation in which a person plants seeds of doubt in the targeted individual, making them question their memory, perception, or judgment. Gaslighting is psychological manipulation to make you question your thinking and make you unsure of a situation's realities. This form of manipulation can be pervasive when you love someone with an addiction. The addict is often in denial about their addiction and quickly blames others for their struggles.

In the book *The Gaslight Effect*, Robert Stern, Ph.D., talks about the danger of letting go of your reality. Stern talks about how gaslighting starts as seemingly minor offences. But the problem is that even tiny instances of questioning your judgment or validity can damage you. An example of gaslighting might be where a drug addict manipulates his partner to make her think she's losing her sense of reality so that his addiction is no longer the focus.

Some techniques a gaslighter uses might be withholding information or pretending they don't understand. The gaslighter might also be countering or changing specific memories or experiences. The gaslighter might also divert or change the subject or question your thinking. The gaslighter also trivializes or makes your needs and feelings seem unimportant. Another technique that the gaslighter might use is denial or forgetting, where the manipulator pretends to have forgotten what has happened or denies something they previously said or did.

Recognizing Gaslighting

How Do You Know When Gaslighting is Happening to You? Whether it's happening with small or big instances, it's essential to be aware of the red flags that you might be a victim of gaslighting. Stern also talks about how the manipulator holds enough power that the gaslighting target is terrified to change the relationship because of the threat of losing that relationship. The bottom line is when someone you love is gaslighting, you want to believe the other person, and the gaslighter might use this against you. It is common even to change your perception to avoid having a conflict. You want to become cautious of gaslighting if you question yourself a lot. Gaslighting can also be more subtle in the form of a simple question like, why are you so sensitive? It's not a big deal. Some examples of gaslighting are

- You're overly sensitive.
- You're crazy.
- Why do you make such a big deal out of things?
- You are nuts. Why do you think I leave?
- It's over with now.

Some Signs That Someone is Gaslighting You: According to Stern, look for these common signs or red flags that will demonstrate that this type of manipulation might be happening to you:

- second-guessing yourself
- trouble making decisions
- questioning your character
- confusion about your relationship
- feeling like you're going crazy
- feeling like your buttons are being pushed
- suddenly finding yourself in an argument
- feeling unclear about your thoughts
- feeling vague about your feelings or beliefs
- notice yourself apologizing
- making excuses for your partner's behaviour
- knowing something is wrong but not sure what

How to avoid the gaslight effect and stay strong emotionally

STEP 1: Noticing: The first step to avoiding the gaslight effect is to notice when it is happening. Take notes about conversations and start journaling to sort out potential distortions.

STEP 2: Feel: Pay attention to how you are feeling. And notice if you're questioning your thoughts, perceptions, or feelings. You have a right to have all the emotions that you have.

STEP 3: Disengage: You have the right not to participate in the gaslight effect. To regain your sense of reality, you might need to disengage. Say things like *how fascinating. Interestingly, you say that. That's not my perception.*

Try using the grey rock method, a tactic some people use when dealing with abusive or manipulative behaviour. It involves becoming as uninteresting and unengaged as possible so that the abusive person loses interest.

STEP 4: Talk to someone: Sometimes, it's beneficial to hear yourself talking and share with others to get another perspective.

STEP 5: Responsibility: Although the behaviour of other people does affect you, it is essential to take responsibility for what you are feeling in the moment and, as you do that, practice self-compassion.

BOUNDARIES AND SELF-RESPECT

Self-respect is important because it is a gift you give yourself. It means you honour yourself and give yourself the gift of approval and regard. Having boundaries for every area of your life is the best description of self-respect. When you respect yourself, you know when to say no to what is no longer emotionally, mentally, or physically healthy for you—and say yes to all those things that energize and lift you. Gaining self-respect is about learning your worth, knowing your value, and advocating for yourself and your needs.

Self-respect is essential because, given this belief, you set boundaries with others and essentially draw the line concerning what you will and will not tolerate. Without self-respect, when you are treated poorly by another person, you will tolerate undeserving and unfair treatment. Self-respect is all about honouring what mistreatment you will not tolerate anymore, bringing an opportunity for better relationships, better self-esteem, and more happiness. You are just as important and worthy as any human being. You deserve loving regard.

Being armed with the knowledge of addictive behaviours and narcissism is empowering. Establishing boundaries is a form of self-respect. Setting your boundaries is essential because they provide you with basic guidelines for how you want to be treated. Establishing boundaries is about setting limits for acceptable behaviours from those around you.

Think of boundaries as limits or rules you set for yourself within relationships. One part of being in a relationship with someone who has an addiction is that your typical boundaries or limits often get overstepped and abused. Boundaries are clear indications of what you desire for yourself and are an act of self-respect.

Boundaries are not strict rules that control other people.

It's important to acknowledge that you must take care of yourself first to have time, energy, and resources to support others. You feel more in control and confident when you have boundaries. It sets you up for success to say no, and you also don't allow others to overwhelm and dictate your happiness.

Establishing boundaries will let you identify your needs, wants, and responsibilities, allowing others to respect you more. It is a reliable, concrete way to say to yourself and show others that we are worthy, deserving, and have needs. Choosing self-respect is about taking the time to consider your feelings and care for your emotional health.

Acknowledge to yourself that you deserve respectful treatment. Avoid allowing anyone to treat you disrespectfully. With boundaries, you're less likely to become entangled in the chaos of addiction, and you will be better able to focus on yourself and your well-being.

SETTING BOUNDARIES

Boundaries are psychological fences between people. Space or barrier that offers protection and that offers guidelines for appropriate behaviours, responsibilities, and actions. When you don't have any boundaries or weak boundaries, you can lose yourself, your freedom, personal space, and self-respect. When you do set boundaries with an addicted loved one, you are not only taking care of yourself but also increasing the chance to seek help. Boundaries give you a sense of control and sanity in the often chaotic and seemingly uncontrollable situation. We all have limits. Think of your boundaries like a no-trespassing sign. Boundaries can be challenging to set, navigate, and communicate. Boundaries are not a one size fits all kind of thing. Here are some tips to consider when building your boundaries.

Steps for Setting Boundaries

Name your limits and where you stand: What are your rights? An example of your rights might be, "I have the right to say no without feeling guilty." "I have the right to be treated with respect." "I have the right to make my needs as important as others." Knowing your rights is a great place to start when setting boundaries. What are your rights?

Tap into your feelings: Determine your values and understand your wants and needs. Follow your gut. Access your wise self or intuition. Boundaries are a personal choice. Your instincts can help you determine when someone is violating your boundaries or when you need to establish new ones. What are your values? Narrow down values to your top 5-10 values. Reflect on what you value and consider making that a part of your boundaries.

- Who are you?
- What do you love?
- What is important to you?

Once you clearly understand what matters most, you can better communicate this to others.

Communicating your boundaries: Be direct and assertive with expressing your boundaries. Be firm but kind. Strong language is clear and non-negotiable, without blame or threat.

Consider using statements like:

I feel _____ (emotion), when _____ (observation) because I _____ (value/need). What I need is _____ (boundary).

Learn to say No: It can be challenging to say no to somebody you love who is struggling. Still, with practice, the assertiveness that comes with this boundary-setting is empowering. Consider that saying "no" is a complete sentence. You can say no without any explanation and see it as a powerful communication method when you feel uncomfortable.

Navigating your boundaries: Permit yourself to make mistakes with setting boundaries; keep practicing. Remember, you cannot change others; you can only change yourself. Boundaries are set for you, not to demand someone else to stop being difficult. Since you can't change other people, change how you deal with them by selecting and adjusting boundaries.

Decide consequences ahead of time: Consider past and present. What do you do when someone inevitably tries to push against your boundaries? Decide the consequences before your boundaries have been tested: Sit down quietly with yourself and list your limits. Remember to honour your needs and values when deciding the consequences of crossing boundaries. After presenting your boundaries clearly to people, let your behaviour do the talking. When tested, pushed, and disrespected, ensure you follow through with the consequences you have decided.

Boundaries can be flexible and adaptable:

1. Don't beat yourself up if boundaries are disrespected and you cannot follow through on consequences.

2. Reestablish new boundaries and, if needed, further consequences.

3. Be gentle with yourself and acknowledge that boundary setting is like a muscle; it takes time to develop.

Sometimes you have to go back to the drawing board and remember why you're setting boundaries in the first place. You might say to yourself, "I set boundaries to feel safe," or "Setting boundaries is an act of self-respect."

Some Boundary Examples:

- You do not allow drug or alcohol use in your home.
- You do not put up with abusive behaviour.
- You do not lend or give them money.
- You don't allow drug-using friends in the house.
- You do not pay off their debts.
- You don't tolerate disappearing.
- You detach when necessary.
- You do not lie or cover up for them.
- You do not allow physical contact if they've been drinking.
- You will not tolerate a friend or family member speaking down to you.
- You will not have others in your home with the kids when you aren't there.

By setting boundaries with others, you allow yourself the necessary room to focus on your own needs and actions you have free space to dedicate to your healing. Setting boundaries can protect you from becoming entangled in others' emotional drama and addiction.

LOVING FROM A DISTANCE BOUNDARY

Sometimes loving someone from a distance is better than having your feelings crushed and your world turned upside down. Keeping distance does not reflect how much you love or care about someone. Detachment is not that you stop loving the person but merely stepping away from the reckless chaos often associated with loving someone with an addiction.

Unfortunately, their behaviour is unlikely to change until the addict decides to do so for themselves. We often sacrifice ourselves to care for them and try to help. Detaching with love is a process of stepping away from an addict so that you can practice self-respect, self-compassion, and self-care. Stepping away allows you to move out of the quicksand and make the most of your own life, even if the addicted person isn't ready or does not want help.

There are a few reasons why it's crucial to love from a distance and detach yourself:

- You could be enabling your loved one's addiction.
- You could be falling into the trap of developing codependency.
- You are not thriving due to the ups and downs associated with addiction.

Detaching with love is the simple step of taking a step back to gain some space for your well-being. You might realize that the person with the addiction will continue to hurt you, and it's about deciding to put yourself first.

Detaching with love is not a question of your level of love but rather about treating yourself with respect while honouring your needs. Of course, you can still communicate and talk with your loved ones and even treat them with respect and love. It is about becoming less emotionally involved in their decisions and their mistakes. It's about not taking responsibility for their actions and saving you.

Loving from a distance is about detaching with love, so you don't play the role of an enabler or a codependent and can focus more on your well-being. Detachment can be complicated, but it is often essential for your well-being.

Taking a step back is one of the ways you choose to put your life back on track so that you can take better care of yourself. Sometimes self-respect is to detach from an addict with love. This step is sometimes easier said than done.

Tips to love from a distance:
1. Stop taking responsibility for the poor choices of your loved one.
2. Relinquish control as you have no power to control their addiction.
3. Stop picking up the slack or paying for their financial mistakes.
4. Stop making excuses for them or defending them.

5. Let go of being in rescue mode, as you can't cure or save your loved one.

6. Put yourself first.

7. Become a matcher. Give and take with reciprocity. Match the levels of giving in others.

8. Remember, you aren't the cause of the behaviour.

9. Claim your happiness because your peace and joy matter.

Living with and loving an addict is never a comfortable experience. Still, by making your self-respect a top priority, setting boundaries, and detaching with love, you will remove yourself from responsibility and be able to regain your power.

KEY TAKE-AWAYS

⊘ Self-respect is holding yourself in esteem and believing you are worthy of being treated well.

⊘ Boundaries are rules or guidelines you can establish to protect your well-being.

⊘ Self-respect has much to do with honouring and acting by your values. Remembering what you value will give you clues as to what is essential to you.

⊘ Enabling refers to the positive act of helping someone accomplish something that they could not do alone. Enabling also refers to helping someone in such a way that rather than solving a problem, it is making a situation worse.

⊘ Codependency often has you funnelling your energy into supporting the people in your life without making space for, or even considering, what you need for yourself.

⊘ Narcissism is when someone has an inflated sense of importance and lacks empathy for others. Narcissism and addiction often go hand and hand.

⊘ Establishing boundaries is a form of self-respect. Setting your boundaries is essential because they provide you with basic guidelines for how you want to be treated. Establishing boundaries is about setting limits for acceptable behaviours from those around you.

CHAPTER REFLECTION QUESTIONS:

Take a moment to write down your highlights from this chapter:

- What takeaways are going to inspire you the most going forward?

  _____

  _____

  _____

  _____

  _____

  _____

- What brought a significant or slight shift in your thinking, feelings, or behaviour?

  _____

  _____

  _____

  _____

  _____

  _____

CHAPTER SIX

You Are Enough:
Dust Off Your Crown and Know Your Worth

"You yourself, as much as anybody in the entire universe, deserve your love and affection." — Buddha

You are enough. Let's tap back into your self-worth. Self-worth is an internal state of being that comes from self-acceptance and self-love. It's a measure of how you value and regard yourself despite what others may say or do. Self-worth and self-value are two related terms used interchangeably. Having a sense of self-worth means that you value yourself, and having a sense of self-value means that you are worthy.

Loving someone with an addiction can quickly erode self-worth. According to the American Psychological Association, having high self-worth is key to positive mental health and well-being. High self-worth matters because it helps you develop coping skills, handle adversity, and put the negative into perspective. A healthy sense of self-worth can improve relationships, work, health, and overall mental and emotional well-being.

In this chapter, you will discover the following:

- What self-worth is, where it comes from and the difference
  between self-worth and self-esteem.
- Barriers to healthy self-worth.
- How to assess and build your self-worth.
- What is self-efficacy, and how does it contribute to self-worth?
- How to conquer self-doubt and build confidence and belief in yourself.

WHAT IS SELF-WORTH?

Self-worth means that you value yourself and sense that you are worthy. It's a general feeling that you are a good person who deserves to be treated with respect. Self-worth is your opinion about yourself and the value you can bring to the world. An example of self-worth may be that you believe you are a good person who deserves good things. Self-worth and self-value are two related terms that are often used interchangeably.

The excellent news about self-worth is that no one can take this away from you. Self-worth comes from a place of self-understanding, self-love and self-acceptance. It's a measure or snapshot of how you value and regard yourself despite what others might say or do.

Similarly, the World Book Dictionary defines self-esteem as "thinking well of oneself; self-respect," while self-worth is defined as "a favourable estimate or opinion of oneself; self-esteem."

Self-worth is self-valuing. Self-worth is also about self-love, and it means being on your team. Here are some key factors or beliefs that go along with self-worth:

- If you have higher self-worth, you believe that no matter what you've done or haven't done, you are worthy of love.
- Material things do not define you.
- You are allowed to feel whatever feelings you are feeling.
- You hold space for your emotions without feeling guilty about them.
- Regardless of being left out or included, you believe in the people who are important in your life.
- You create time and space for yourself and honour that by setting firm boundaries.

- It's not about what happened; it's about how you respond to what happens.
- A self-worthy person puts their needs first and often seeks win-win situations.

SELF-ESTEEM AND SELF-WORTH

Self-esteem is what we think, feel, and believe about ourselves. Self-worth is knowing deeply that you have value, are lovable, and are necessary to contribute to this life and world. Self-esteem and self-worth are two different things. Self-esteem is easy to lose, whereas self-worth is empowering and in your control.

The main difference is that you can have self-esteem and think you're good at something and still not feel convinced that you are loveable or worthy. People with low self-esteem are consistently afraid of making mistakes or letting others down. Self-worth goes deeper and has a more significant impact. Self-esteem is more about feeling good about yourself. But the question then becomes, what happens when we don't feel good about ourselves?

Instead of focusing on just feeling good about yourself, it is more beneficial to know your self-worth. Self-worth is a deep understanding of who you are as a person. When you go through a struggle and challenge, it's easy to lose self-esteem. If you have a sense of self-worth, it helps you thrive when you go through a challenge. Your value is not based on someone else's bad behaviour or evaluation of you.

You have deep infinite worth. In the book The Self-Worth Safari, John Niland explains the difference as: "Self-esteem is a bit like walking down the street as if you owned it. Self-worth is walking down the street and not caring who owns it." Self-worth is self-love. Your worth does not decrease based on someone's inability to see your value.

WHY SELF-WORTH IS IMPORTANT

There are several reasons why self-worth is essential for health and happiness. Essentially, it helps you to love and respect yourself.

- It allows you to create personal boundaries.
- It enables you to be confident. It will let you be authentic.
- It helps you to remove toxic people and habits from your life.
- It inspires you to find loving friends and partners.
- The consequences of low self-worth can be devastating.

- Low self-worth is associated with depression, anxiety, the willingness to tolerate abuse, and a nagging sense of defeat.

The great news is that you can do things to increase your self-worth so you can show up and be on your team and your best cheerleader, especially when you're going through challenges in your life, such as loving someone with an addiction.

Since self-worth comes from a place where you have a sense of your value or worth, it naturally builds your sense of self-efficacy. Self-efficacy refers to your own belief in your capacity to deal with things necessary in your life. When you have self-efficacy, it reflects confidence in your ability to influence your environment significantly. When you love someone with an addiction, your life can feel very much out of control. Although powerless over someone else's addiction, you still have value and worth to offer this world. You can still build your self-efficacy.

Albert Bandura, psychologist and author of Social Learning Theory, has defined self-efficacy as one's belief in one's ability to succeed in specific situations or accomplish a task. One's sense of self-efficacy can play a significant role in approaching goals, tasks, and challenges. It forms a firmer stance on your worth and taking the initiative in your life. It allows you to recover more quickly from setbacks and disappointment, and you can view challenging problems as tasks you can overcome.

When all else seems lost, if you increase your sense of self-worth and self-efficacy, you are more likely to thrive and become resilient, even amongst some of the biggest challenges or setbacks. You will also be more confident in yourself, gain faith in your ability to handle what life throws at us, become more self-reliant, regain spirit, and gain belief in yourself and self-worth.

BARRIERS TO SELF-WORTH

Your self-worth can be influenced by your beliefs on the type of person you are, what you can do, your strengths, weaknesses, and future expectations. There may be particular people in your life whose messages about you can also contribute to your self-worth and affect your self-esteem. Knowing some barriers to self-worth, you can better work with those obstacles to regain your power.

Self-Doubt: Low self-esteem is when someone lacks confidence about who they are and what they can do. They often feel incompetent, unloved, or inadequate. Self-doubt and the inner critic is the voice inside your head reminding you that you are "not good enough." It's behind the insidious thoughts that can make you second-guess your every action and doubt your value. The inner critic might feel overpowering, but you can manage it effectively. Self-doubt and the inner critic are barriers to self-worth.

In the book, *Make Peace with Your Mind*, meditation teacher and therapist Mark Coleman helps readers understand and free themselves from the inner critic using mindfulness and compassion tools. In his book, Coleman says the inner critic is like a lousy accountant who only looks at the column in red, or the liabilities, without considering the assets. The inner critic can erode all sense of self-worth.

Self-Judgment: There is an epidemic of self-judgment, and the critic shows up everywhere, especially when presented with challenging situations. Neuroplasticity and the power of choice make it possible to rewire the brain and regain control of this inner critic or negative self-talk. The words you speak do not determine your life. What you whisper to yourself in your head has the most power. Your brain is simply coding, and you can change that programming. Mindfulness allows you to choose what you pay attention to, which can change the structure of your brain.

Feel Unloveable: Do you catch yourself thinking you are unlovable or unworthy? It's important to note that your value doesn't decrease based on someone else's inability to see your worth. Your value doesn't decrease based on what you do or don't do, have or don't have. The bottom line is that you are worthy and have value to offer this world.

Second-Guessing: Self-doubt creates repetitive negative thinking and second-guessing and makes our situation seem even worse than it potentially is. When you constantly doubt yourself and your decisions, you start to feel like you don't have control over your life. Second-guessing can lead to depression, lowered self-esteem and self-worth.

Negative Thinking: Negative thinking refers to thinking negatively about yourself and your surroundings. Negative thought includes negative beliefs you might have about yourself, situations, or others. Negative thinking can contribute to problems such as social anxiety, depression, stress, and low self-worth. Our thoughts, emotions, and behaviours are all linked, so our thoughts impact how we feel and act.

Lack of Self-Efficacy: People with low self-efficacy view difficult tasks as personal threats and shy away from them. Difficult tasks lead them to look at the skills they need to improve rather than the ones they have. It is easy to lose faith in your abilities after a failure if you lack self-efficacy and are deficient in believing in yourself and your abilities. Self-worth comes from a realistic respect for your ability to achieve and thrive, while self-efficacy is how you feel about your ability to function in different situations. If you lack self-efficacy, you tend to be more hopeless and may question your self-worth.

Self-worth comes from a place where you have a sense of your value or worth. Low self-worth is like being a tree without roots. You bend and fall when the wind blows and when faced with challenging situations. Building your self-worth contributes to your self-confidence and makes you robust in facing challenges. If you struggle to feel good about yourself, you're not alone. Self-worth means believing that you are fundamentally a worthy person. You have inherent value and many strengths. The excellent news is that you can develop, learn, and strengthen your self-worth. Let's first look at the significant contributor to the barriers to self-worth: self-doubt.

REFLECTION QUESTION:

- What might be some of your barriers to self-worth?

ASSESS YOUR SELF-WORTH

What does NOT determine your inherent value or self-worth, and what does? Read through the list below and assess your self-worth. You might have to dig deeper to find what contributes to your self-worth. Self-esteem-boosting things scream louder and are apparent.

Find your inherent value. Write in your journal.

What should NOT determine your inherent value:

- Your to-do list.
- Your job.
- Your social media following.
- Your age.
- Flattery.
- Material possessions.
- How far you jog.
- The marks that you get at school.
- Your relationship status.
- How much money you have in the bank.
- Other people.

What is your inherent value or worth?

Here are some statements that might get you started:

- No matter what I have done or haven't done, I am worthy of love.
- The things in my life do not define me.
- I am allowed to feel whatever it is I am feeling.
- I take responsibility for my mistakes, "I did a bad thing" instead of "I am bad."
- It's not about what happens; it's about how I respond to what happens.
- I put my own needs first.
- I create space for my emotions without feeling guilty.
- I can be considerate of others.
- I make time and space just for myself.
- I honour my boundaries.
- I find joy in doing what I love.
- I lean on loved ones for support.
- I connect to what I value most in life.
- I listen to my truth.
- I am a part of something greater and never alone.
- I see opportunities to learn and grow.
- I accept myself and others.
- I am thankful for the challenges in my life.
- I am learning and growing.
- Every day, I find something to be grateful for.

- Even amidst challenges, I can see things I can be thankful for.
- I influence the way I live.

REFLECTION QUESTIONS:

- What boosts your self-esteem?
- What is your inherent value?

WHAT IS SELF-DOUBT?

When you go through a challenge, it is common to start second-guessing your worth and experience a struggle to be good enough. It is common to move into self-doubt when you love someone with an addiction. When you feel knocked down, it becomes essential to build general confidence and unwavering belief in yourself. Knowing your worth can help you persevere in facing setbacks, criticism, and challenge.

Your thoughts and beliefs about yourself and your abilities could be very different from the reality of the situation, regardless of feedback, evidence, and experience. You could be doing well and fully capable, thinking you are not good enough and held back by self-doubt, shame, or unworthy thinking. Self-doubt creates repetitive negative thinking and second-guessing and makes our situation seem even worse than it potentially is.

Self-doubt is a general sense of feeling unsure about one's competencies, abilities, and outcomes in daily life. Self-doubt is socially constructed, meaning you value what others think about you. You can see how you could potentially be significantly affected by the addicted loved one in your life that is abusive, manipulative, and mean. You could start to believe the insults they spew out when they feel down or need the next fix. To sum up, low self-worth is a product of fear and a fundamental misunderstanding about who you are and the strength that you bring.

REFLECTION QUESTION:

- Where and how has self-doubt crept into your life?

CONQUER SELF-DOUBT

In the book *Wire Your Brain For Confidence: The Science of Conquering Self-Doubt*, Positive Psychology expert Louisa Jewell walks you through some tips to help you build your self-worth and rewire your brain for confidence. Here are some of her suggestions and key takeaways from her book:

Say yes when the brain says no: Try new things that build your confidence and boost a sense of self-efficacy or belief in yourself.

Think of you at your best: Science shows that people that believe in their abilities act, think, and feel differently. Put more effort into achieving your goals.

Build your confidence muscle: To build your self-efficacy and courage to act, build up your skills with practice (get better at something), set mini-learning goals, learn, and get better.

Fail forward: Recognize when you fail at something and decide to learn and grow instead of judging yourself. Don't let failure determine your worth.

Seeing is believing: Find role models or people who have been in your shoes or gone before you that can help you learn, grow, and feel encouraged. Visualize the peaceful life you desire for yourself.

Surround yourself with the right people:
1. Choose to be around uplifting, encouraging people.
2. Nurture your growth mindset.
3. Be curious to learn and grow.

Care less about what people think about you: Be open to constructive feedback but limit (as much as possible) exposure to toxic relationships and people.

Use your body and emotions as power: When you stand tall and take up space, your posture is a power pose. Use body positivity to boost your self-worth and focus on functionality instead of what it looks like to you.

REFLECTION QUESTIONS:

- What will you apply to your life right away?
- What resonates with you the most from this list?

BUILDING CONFIDENCE AND BELIEF IN YOURSELF

Self-Worth is the recognition that you are a valuable human worthy of love. Self-Confidence, on the other hand, is the degree to which you trust in yourself and your ability to deal with challenges, solve problems, and engage successfully with the world. You can see how they go hand in hand. Confidence helps you feel ready for life's experiences. When confident, you're more likely to move forward with people and opportunities instead of backing away.

And if things don't work out, confidence helps you to try again. When you have more self-worth, you have greater confidence. Both are essential for regaining your power.

Believing in yourself and your ability to struggle well through the trauma associated with loving someone with addiction becomes essential. When facing a challenge, we need to rise instead of giving up and being defeated. Confidence influences your thoughts, actions, emotions, and even motivation. It becomes your backbone as it affects almost every aspect of your well-being. Psychologists even believe it's vital to help people realize their self-worth and power through life's challenges.

In the book, *The Confidence Code*, Katty Kay and Claire Shipman talk about self-assurance, science and art. They explain that confidence has a family consisting of self-worth, optimism, self-compassion, and self-efficacy. Self-worth allows you to believe that you are lovable and have value as a human being. Optimism causes you to expect the most favourable outcome from any given situation, which breeds confidence and the sense that everything will work out.

Gaining confidence means getting outside your comfort zone, experiencing setbacks, and regaining yourself.

When you love someone with an addiction, setbacks and challenges seem to be around every corner. Whether you are still on the rollercoaster or have jumped off, your confidence might need some loving attention. Here are some suggestions based on scientific research to boost your confidence muscle:

The starting point for risk, failure, perseverance, and ultimately, confidence is a way of thinking defined by Stanford Psychology Professor Carol Dweck as a "growth mindset." She has found that the most successful and fulfilled people believe they can improve and learn things. A growth mindset builds self-compassion, self-efficacy, self-worth, and optimism. Confidence requires a growth mindset because thinking you can learn skills leads to doing new things. It encourages risk and supports resilience when you fail or face setbacks. When you adopt a growth mindset through practice, you can improve and build your confidence.

Build a Confidence Growth Mindset:
- Adopting a willingness to be different (authentic) is critical to confidence.
- Choose confidence.
- Be adaptive.
- Practice quick failures.
- Make repeated attempts.

- Try something you've meant to try.
- When in doubt, take action.
- Step out of your comfort zone.
- What's the worst that could happen? That's right - you could fail.
- Practice self-compassion. "Yes, sometimes I do fail, we all fail, and that's okay."
- Don't ruminate.
- Negate ANTs(Automatic Negative Thoughts).
- Become purpose-driven.
- Don't take it personally.
- Find ways to absorb compliments.
- Speak up.
- Praise progress, not perfection.
- Be honest, kind, and firm.

To reclaim your power, looking at the barriers to self-worth while building confidence is imperative for regaining your power.

SELF-EFFICACY: A SECRET INGREDIENT FOR SELF-WORTH

In psychology, self-efficacy is an individual's belief in their capacity to act in the ways necessary to reach specific goals and the worthiness to do so. You can build, maintain and improve self-efficacy. Self-efficacy's goal-oriented nature is the key to putting aspirations into action and knowing your strength to try. If you have a strong sense of self-efficacy, you will look at challenges as tasks to be conquered; you will be more deeply involved in the activities you take on, and you will recover faster from setbacks.

Albert Bandura is a contemporary psychologist specializing in developmental psychology. Much of his work centers around social learning theory. As Dr. Albert Bandura puts it, self-efficacy significantly contributes to human well-being and functioning. The foundation of success and human flourishing is self-efficacy. Here are some tips from positive psychology researchers on how to work to increase your self-efficacy.

How to Build, Maintain, and Improve Self-Efficacy:

Notice Success and Accept Failure: Self-mastery requires resilience to manage expectations and accept failure as an opportunity to learn and grow. As you keep overcoming obstacles, you gain strength and self-belief. Accept failures and criticism positively. Everyday practice and eventual mastery is a big way to build belief in yourself and self-worth.

Role Models and Examples: Role models or others that have been through something similar and gotten through it make you feel like you are not alone and give you confidence that you will be okay. Seeing others accomplish or overcome challenges can help build confidence that we can get through things. Avoid comparison and surround yourself with positive and supportive people that help you believe in yourself.

Be Nice to Yourself: Self-compassion and kind understanding towards yourself help you gain self-efficacy. You lower your self-efficacy when you are rude and overly critical towards yourself. Be on your team and believe in yourself. Focus on your successes and mini accomplishments instead of your shortcomings. Pay attention to your self-talk.

Focus on Your Strength:
1. Focus more on your strengths rather than your weaknesses.
2. Rejoice even in your small successes.
3. Maximize your abilities and use your strengths.

Stretch Yourself:
1. Set goals and move away from apathy (comfort zone) and towards your goals.

2. Stay in a positive environment and make the most of your abilities.

3. Persevere and try new things and face small challenges.

4. Think about starting a passion project or a new class. What makes you excited? What do you want to try?

5. Maximize your effort even amongst challenges.

Avoid Familiar Stressful Situations: Adversity affects your well-being and performance. Notice the particular places or people that take you down. When you can, go someplace else, be with other people, or practice being responsive, like a grey stone. One strategy for dealing with difficult people is to act like a "grey stone," meaning you become less interested and more unresponsive. You don't feed their need for drama or attention. You don't show emotion or say anything that could be argued.

Reframe Obstacles: Reconstruct how you look at failure and think instead about how you can apply positive interventions to blocks, challenges, and setbacks. Going through the difficulties of loving someone with an addiction is not a loss or personal shortcoming. It is essential to try to cope with it and find ways to handle things.

REFLECTION QUESTIONS:

- What does self-efficacy mean to you?
- How will you build your self-efficacy?

CULTIVATE MORE SELF-WORTH

- Boost Your Self-Acceptance
- Enhance Your Self-Love
- Recognize Your Worth
- Recognize What You're Good At
- Conquer Self-Doubt
- Give Yourself a Challenge
- Take Responsibility For Your Needs
- Learn To Be Assertive
- Practice Mindfulness and Self-Awareness
- Build Positive Relationships
- Identify Negative Thoughts
- Replace Negative Thoughts

THE POWER OF POSITIVE SELF-TALK

Self-talk is something that we do naturally throughout our entire day. It is an internal dialogue that you have with yourself. Self-talk can be both damaging and optimistic at the same time, as well as encouraging or distracting. It can build up your self-worth or erode it. That inner voice that provides a running dialogue may or may not be in your awareness. This internal narrative is a constant chatter inside your head that may or may not be accurate.

Negative self-talk is something that people experience from time to time, and it can contribute to a significant amount of stress if you are not careful. Negative self-talk isn't good for you because this internal dialogue can significantly limit your ability to believe in yourself and your capabilities of navigating your life.

Both negative and positive self-talk can create a self-fulfilling prophecy. A self-fulfilling prophecy is a prediction that comes true, at least partly due to a person's beliefs or expectations. It is easy to find evidence to support your thinking. The question becomes, what do you want to make a reality for yourself? Negative thinking might be exaggerated, cause rumination and self-blame and can lead to general mental instability. Negative self-talk also lowers your ability to see opportunities and develops limited thinking. Positive self-talk has the power to turn your attention to possibilities and opportunities. Positive self-talk helps you focus on solution thinking and tap into your strengths, abilities and resources. Positive self-talk enhances your self-worth, self-efficacy, and confidence.

Ways to Mininmize negative self talk and power up your positive self-tak:

Catch your critic and identify negative self-talk traps.

Acknowledge the negative self-talk first.

Consider what is causing the negative self-talk.

Remember, your thoughts are not always accurate.

Notice if perfection is playing a role.

Change negatives to more neutral self-talk, such as "this is challenging" instead of "I can't do this."

Be like your best friend.

Stop the thought by actually saying, "Stop."

Acknowledge, delete, and cancel, then replace with a better-feeling thought or wording.

Change self-limiting statements to questions: "This is impossible." versus. "How can I handle this?"

Adopt a growth mindset with curiosity.

Notice judgment and move to become a learner.

Give yourself positive affirmations or affirm yourself.

Build or create a positive self-talk routine.

Challenge the negative self-talk with statements like "that's not true because _____." Or "Another way of seeing this is _____."

Create a new positive self-talk statement.

_____

_____

_____

_____

_____

_____

_____

NEGATE AUTOMATIC NEGATIVE THOUGHTS (ANTS):

Most negative thinking is automatic (Automatic Negative Thoughts ANTS) and goes unnoticed. I'm so disappointed in myself. I've let people down. I don't think I can go on. I wish I were a better person. Negative automatic thoughts are the kind of negative self-talk that appears immediately, without us even being aware of forming a thought, in response to a particular stimulus.

Cognitive biases and distortions are sneaky ways in which your mind convinces you of something false. Your brain fools you into thinking that your negative thoughts are accurate and logical, but, in reality, they only reinforce negative thinking and emotions. Psychologists recognize an abundance of cognitive biases. They're often irrational and damaging to your mental well-being.

Here are some different types of (ANTs) Automatic Negative Thoughts:

All-or-nothing thinking: You see things in black-and-white categories.

Overgeneralization: You see a single negative event as a never-ending pattern of defeat.

Mental filter: You pick out a single negative detail and dwell on it.

Disqualifying the positive: You reject positive experiences by insisting they "don't count" for some reason or other. In this way, you can maintain a negative belief.

Jumping to conclusions: You make a negative interpretation even though no definite facts convincingly support your conclusion. It could be mind-reading or fortune-telling.

Magnification (catastrophizing) or minimization: You exaggerate the importance of things, or you inappropriately shrink things.

Emotional reasoning: You assume that your negative emotions necessarily reflect how things are: "I feel it; therefore, it must be true."

Should statements: You try to motivate yourself with should and shouldn't. "Musts" and "oughts" are also offenders.

Labelling and mislabelling: This is an extreme form of overgeneralization. Instead of describing your error, you attach a negative label to yourself. "I'm a loser."

Blaming: Realize that you are responsible for your actions, thoughts, and attitudes.

Personalization: You see yourself as the cause of some adverse external event you were not primarily responsible for."

Automatic negative thoughts can become overwhelmingly stressful but can be overcome with simple techniques to challenge and control them. Being self-aware is the first step.

When you recognize an automatic negative thought, ask yourself questions like these:

- Is this thought true?
- Does having this thought serve me?
- Is there another explanation or another way of looking at things?
- What advice would I give to a friend who had this thought?

REFLECTION QUESTIONS:

- What are your typical ANTS?
- How are these thoughts serving you?
- Is there another way of looking at things?

WHAT TO SAY WHEN YOU TALK TO YOURSELF

When you talk to yourself, or you are thinking, you want to make sure it is in a way that builds up your self-worth.

Self-talk is the internal narrative you hold about yourself. It's your inner voice. Your self-talk can significantly influence how you see yourself and the world around you more than you realize. One powerful way is to affirm your worth in a way that feels honest and empowering. But what do you say when you talk to yourself? It's important to know that not everyone's positive self-talk will be the same. Try a few different approaches to find the ones that ultimately work for you.

Your mind is a powerful thing. Affirmations are potent expressions of self-talk that can build up your self-worth. You can say, think, and hear them and reap the benefits of positive self-talk. Affirmations are like sentences that help with your thinking patterns, habits, and self-worth. Affirmations are motivating; they change how you think, what you focus on, and your behaviour, making you feel more optimistic. Affirmations are positive statements that can help you to challenge and overcome self-sabotaging and negative thoughts. When you repeat them often and believe in them, you can start to make positive changes.

Affirmations have the power to

- Motivate you to act on certain things.
- Help you to concentrate on achieving your goals in life.

- Give you the ability to change negative thinking patterns and replace them with positive ones.
- Assist you in accessing a new belief system.
- Reaffirm the positivity back into your life.
- Help regain or increase your self-confidence and self-worth.

Do you still need to figure out the power of affirmations? Try the brighter side experiment to show yourself the power of what you focus your attention on and the effects.

THE BRIGHTER SIDE EXPERIMENT:

STEP 1: Next time you are in public, take five minutes to notice everything you don't like. Notice how you feel. Then take the next five minutes to see everything you do like, everything positive and uplifting or beautiful. Notice how you feel. Simply shifting your attention to what is uplifting, good, and positive directly impacts your state of mind and heart at that moment. That is how powerful affirmations or focused self-talk can have on your well-being.

STEP 2: Now, do the same thing with yourself. Focus on all the things you like and appreciate about yourself. Reflect on your accomplishments, gifts, and positive qualities. Call to mind the kind or generous things you have done. Appreciate your body and all it does for you. Affirm to yourself your worth.

Creating your affirmations:

Practicing positive affirmations can be extremely simple: pick a phrase and repeat it yourself. You may use positive affirmations to motivate yourself, encourage positive changes in your life, or boost your self-esteem.

The formula for writing effective affirmations:
1. Write in the first person.
2. Write in the positive (as opposed to the negative).
3. Make sure it has an emotional charge.
4. Write in the present state.

Here are a few examples of affirmations to get you started:

- I prioritize my well-being and consider what truly serves me with each decision.
- I have the power to change my mind.
- I forgive myself for being imperfect because I am human. Every perceived failure provides an opportunity to learn and grow.
- Even though it wasn't the outcome I hoped for, I learned a lot about myself.

- I feel amazing when I wake up early, dedicate a few moments to myself, and move my body. I am committed to this habit and proud of myself for upholding it.
- I can't control what other people think, say or do. I can only control myself.
- My goals are valid, and I am equipped to achieve them. I believe in myself and take the necessary daily steps to fulfill my dreams.
- I believe in my strength. Every day I am learning from my challenges.
- I am a good person and worthy of love. I forgive myself for not being perfect.
- This is an opportunity for me to try something new.
- I am stronger than I think I am. I am enough, and I am loveable.
- Every day, in every way, I am getting better and better.
- I make the world a brighter place.
- I am liberating myself from fear, judgment, and doubt.

REFLECTION QUESTIONS:

- What are your affirmations?
- When is a good time to affirm?

KEY TAKE-AWAYS

✓ Self-worth means that you value yourself and sense that you are worthy. It's a general feeling that you are a good person who deserves to be treated with respect.

✓ Self-esteem is what we think, feel, and believe about ourselves. Self-worth is knowing deeply that you have value, are lovable, are necessary to this life, and have worth.

✓ Your self-worth can be influenced by your beliefs about the type of person you are, what you can do, your strengths, weaknesses, and future expectations.

✓ When you go through a challenge, it is common to start second-guessing your worth and struggle to be good enough. It is common to move into self-doubt when you love someone with an addiction.

✓ In psychology, self-efficacy is an individual's belief in their capacity to act in the ways necessary to reach specific goals and the worthiness to do so.

✓ Self-talk is something that we do naturally throughout our entire day. It is an internal dialogue that you have with yourself. Self-talk can be damaging and optimistic and can be encouraging or distracting. It can build up your self-worth or erode it.

CHAPTER REFLECTION QUESTIONS:

Take a moment to write down your highlights from this chapter:

- What takeaways are going to inspire you the most going forward?

_____

_____

_____

_____

_____

_____

- What brought a significant or slight shift in your thinking, feelings, or behaviour?

_____

_____

_____

_____

_____

_____

CHAPTER SEVEN

You Deserve Self-Care:
Make Yourself Feel Safe, Healthy, and Calm

"An empty lantern provides no light. Self-care is the fuel that allows your light to shine brightly." — Adage.

Self-care is about doing things to look after your emotional, psychological, spiritual, and physical health. Good self-care is the key to well-being. To regain your power and save yourself, you need to take care of your own needs and not sacrifice your well-being for others. If you allow people to make more withdrawals than deposits in your life, you will become depleted in no time. Self-care means caring for your whole self. Self-care allows you to maintain a healthy relationship with yourself to be resilient. An example of self-care might be going for a walk, drinking water or practicing good sleep hygiene.

So why should you love and care for yourselves? Whether going to your favourite spa, relaxing in a yoga class, or just allowing some time to rest in bed, 'me time' is required to rest, recharge, pause, and take stock of your life mindfully. Self-care is a beautiful support tool that you can use to grow, evolve, and expand who you are, and it ultimately makes you feel good about yourself on all levels.

In this chapter, you will understand the following:
- What self-care is and why it is essential for regaining your power.
- The potential obstacles to self-care.
- How to use self-care for healing, coping and well-being.
- Specific tools to foster safety and calm through self-care.

WHAT IS SELF-CARE?

Self-care is deliberately taking care of your mental, emotional, and physical health. Self-care is key to improving your well-being and regulating your nervous system. Loving someone with an addiction can be very stressful. All too often, you put the needs of the addict in your life ahead of your own. When you play the role of caretaker, rescuer, or supporter, you often deplete your resources. It is common for your personal needs and self-care to get pushed aside. But you need self-care practices more than ever when you love someone with an addiction or have lost someone to addiction.

Loving someone with an addiction is exhausting, draining, and even debilitating. Self-care is about performing a conscious act to promote your well-being. Self-care involves focusing on yourself, loving yourself and taking time to rest, reflect, replenish, and renew yourself. It's about taking stock of your own needs. Self-care and self-love are close relatives. The two of them are equally essential but slightly different. Self-care is about taking care of yourself physically, mentally, emotionally and spiritually, whereas self-love means showing kindness towards yourself. You can see how they go hand and hand.

The damaging effects of addiction aren't just the addiction itself; it's the fact that the focus becomes on caring for them, that your needs have been coming in second. You may neglect yourself, and your self-care needs to help the addicted loved one. Chances are loving someone with an addiction has taken a toll on your well-being. Loving someone with an addiction is an enormous cause of stress: sleepless nights, worrying, inconsistency in your life, feelings of hopelessness and sadness, as well as anger and frustration. Stress plays a role in the decline of well-being. Self-care becomes essential to regain your power.

Self-care lowers the impact of dis-stress: The time, energy, and concern put towards the addicted loved ones can deplete your resources and strain your life. It becomes crucial to increase your level of self-care. Self-care is about actively using coping strategies and skills to improve your well-being and manage your life. Science has shown that self-care can lower the negative impact of current and past stress, also known as damage control. It also can reduce the adverse effects of future stress, known as prevention.

Self-care is essential to your well-being: Self-care involves basic human necessities that you can cultivate and nurture at any time. It is about confidence, warmth, caring regard, acceptance of who and what you are, and showing it. Self-care involves taking the necessary steps to look after yourself and loving all aspects of yourself by accepting your flaws and weaknesses and valuing your strengths. It is sometimes initially thought of as selfish, but improving your well-being makes you better able to help your loved one needing support.

Self-care is about slowing down and restoring.

You can't keep pushing: When you push yourself to the maximum and don't practice self-care, you can experience a sense of burnout, ego depletion, and compassion fatigue. These results are widespread among people in a relationship with someone with an addiction. What happens is you can no longer maintain a level of caring or interest because your resources become depleted. Thankfully there are ways that you can help yourself when you love someone with an addiction. Addiction is a disease that affects the entire family. It is easy to become entangled in a world full of worry, frustration, and pain. Self-care is critical for you and the addicted loved one in your life.

WHY SELF-CARE IS IMPORTANT FOR REGAINING YOUR POWER

Taking care of yourself is extremely important in day-to-day living, let alone when dealing with the stress of loving someone with an addiction. Taking time to look after yourself can also remind others that you and your needs are essential. As mentioned earlier in this book, the expression: "you can't pour from an empty cup." Self-care is what is going to fill your cup so that you can give from your reserves. Refrain from emptying your cup.

Self-care is critical to maintaining positive feelings; it boosts your confidence and helps you be optimistic about your future. Self-care is also essential to maintain a healthy relationship with yourself. It does produce positive feelings, and it is necessary to remind yourself and others that you are important. Self-care is a component of stress management. While small doses of stress are healthy for you to meet deadlines or finish tasks, chronic stress and anxiety can adversely affect your mental and physical health. More on dis-stress to come in this chapter.

> *"Remember that everything good you do for*
> *yourself is an act of self love." — Unknown*

EGO DEPLETION AND SELF-REGULATION

The perpetual rollercoaster can become exhausting and depleting when you love someone with an addiction. In positive psychology, a scientific term that describes this state is when you have limited mental resources; it is called ego depletion. Think about how you feel after a busy day full of demands, physically and emotionally. Your energy is not the same as at the beginning of the day. Your choices at the end of the day may not be as good as the choices at the beginning.

In the book *Self-Regulation and Ego Control*, Edward R. Hirt teaches that you find yourself exhausted and burnt out because you are influenced by what psychologists refer to as the ego-depletion effect. When you are depleted, your self-regulation or ability to display willpower, motivation, and emotions is hindered. Because self-management and self-regulation take a lot of effort when you are exhausted, it's harder to practice self-control and self-care. You have little or nothing left when you are depleted and your mental capacity is exhausted. You can see how loving someone with an addiction and all the challenges can be emotionally and physically draining—leaving you with ego depletion and lacking self-regulation or the desire for self-care.

Self-control and self-regulation are beneficial for many reasons, but your well-being will be affected if you lack self-control and self-care. Self-regulation is a vital skill that helps you make decisions in certain situations. It is the control you have over yourself and your choices. According to self-regulation theory expert Roy Baumeister, someone with good self-regulation can keep emotions in check and make thoroughly considered behaviours while sticking to goals and appropriate motivation.

When you have good self-regulation, you gain control over your behaviour and life. Baumeister reports that self-regulation is about having standards of conduct, motivation to meet standards, monitoring situations and thoughts, and willpower that allows internal strength and control of urges. Ego depletion gets in the way of self-regulation. You can see why it becomes essential to prevent or minimize ego depletion. Self-care is critical to avoid ego depletion.

Many things contribute to ego depletion, making it harder to regain power and footing. Loving someone with an addiction often brings emotional distress, unfamiliarity, uncertainty, fatigue, sleep deprivation, less self-control, and stress, all of which contribute to ego depletion. Science has shown that ego depletion can significantly:

- Impact your behaviour and ability to self-regulate.
- Sabotage your willpower, motivation, and desire to be with others.
- Impact on your food choices, your decision-making, and your performance.

So what can you do to minimize the effect of this drain to take back your power?

Research has shown that people are encouraged to practice self-care to prevent ego depletion.

Self-care can build up your ability to self-regulate and contribute to your well-being. Life is a precious gift. It is important to remember that taking care of yourself is also part of your many responsibilities. Self-care is also vital for better physical health; it's about your eating habits, getting enough sleep, caring about your hygiene, and regularly exercising and moving your body.

Many psychological studies have shown that self-care is the foundational key to mental health and well-being and is essential to keep depression and anxiety at bay. Self-care prevents ego depletion and the adverse effects it can cause in our lives. Self-care can put you in a position to better care for yourself and your life. Let's look into various ways to care for yourself and make it a priority.

THE STRESS LOOP

In the book *Burnout: The Secret to Solving the Stress Cycle*, Emily Nagoski and Amelia Nagoski teach the importance of finishing the stress cycle and closing the loop. The stress cycle starts by releasing the hormone epinephrine to push blood into the muscles. As a result, your blood pressure and heart rate go up, your muscles tense, and your breath quickens. This happens all so you can run! Or, as they say in their book, "Haul-Ass away from the theoretical charging rhino."

Body functions, such as growth, digestion, reproduction, and immunity, are all slowed down. When the emotion of stress becomes chronic and never-ending or distressing, the damage and dangers are evident: chronic high blood pressure, higher risk of heart disease, compromised immune and digestive system, slower healing, and higher risk of digestion-related illnesses. They suggest that people close the stress cycle as often as possible to avoid these dangers. That means knowing how to calm down after a stress surge. Stress is about running for your life. The natural ending to this cycle is that you arrive home safely after running for your life.

Close the stress loop: Authors Emily Nagoski and Amelia Nagoski suggest closing the stress cycle by running, swimming, biking, dancing, or engaging in any other blood-pumping exercise for 20-60 minutes. They also suggest shifting your mood and mimicking a safe return home full of calm, soothing, and safety. Alternatively, creative expression, such as painting, and social interactions signal a return to safety. So does affection, deep breathing, and peaceful music. There is a whole host of practices to downregulate the nervous system to duplicate this message of a safe return home.

Downregulate the nervous system: Deep breathing, relaxation techniques, and meditation can help to ease anxiety and nervousness. Down-regulation occurs when you are able to take yourself out of a stress response (often called fight-flight or freeze) and move into a more calm and peaceful place. Downregulation is bringing the system back into balance after the dis-stress. How to calm your overstimulated nervous system:

- Exercise
- Yoga
- Meditation
- Listen to calm music
- Walk in nature
- Sit in nature
- Massage
- Emotional Freedom Technique (EFT tapping is a combination of ancient Chinese acupressure and modern psychology, now known as energy psychology. It's an easy-to-learn technique that involves "tapping" on the meridian points of the body while repeating statements that help us focus on an issue from which we're seeking relief.)
- Havening (Havening refers to a newer alternative therapy technique that incorporates distraction, touch, and eye movements)
- Self-soothing
- Aromatherapy
- Sleep or nap
- Avoid triggers
- Warm blanket
- Play and have fun
- Deep breathing

- Spend time with friends
- Breathwork

The upside to stress: Keep in mind not all stress is bad. Stressful situations and environments may prompt you to be resourceful and flexible and to learn strategies that help you overcome adversity and thrive. Low-to-moderate stress challenges you, potentially leading to growth experiences. Slightly adverse experiences make you stronger and prepare you for future uncertainty. Some stress is psychologically beneficial, potentially acting as a kind of inoculation against developing mental health issues.

REFLECTION QUESTIONS:

- How will you close the stress loop?
- What would mimic a safe return home for you?
- How has stress helped you?

THE POWER OF PLAY AND JOY OF MOVEMENT

Humans are hardwired to take pleasure in the activities, experiences, and mental states that help them survive. Physical activity - whether through exercise, exploration, play, competition, or celebration - makes you happier.

Play, joy, and fun are essential to your well-being and the fabric of your life.

The Power of Play: Play activities are enjoyable and spontaneous about exploration, experimentation, and imitation. In the book *The Power of Play: Optimize Your Joy Potential*, Dr. Elaine O'Brien and myself talk about how play is a time to forget about stress, work and commitments, to be social, and to have unstructured time to enjoy life. Even amongst struggle, you can and should experience moments of joy. For adults, play can provide a release, a mood boost, and a chance to reset. Play provides you with happy moments, rich memories, and a feeling of pleasurable anticipation for the future. Play safeguards your mental health. Here's what science says about the power of play:

- Play contributes to robust health in a number of ways.
- Play creates eustress that keeps you feeling vital and alive.
- Play lowers distress and aggression.
- Play helps facilitate learning in people of all ages.
- Play keeps us sharp.
- Play improves brain function.
- Play is vital for healthy brain development.
- Play stimulates the mind and enhances creativity.

- Play broadens our perspective, helps us build positive resources, and stimulates our imagination.
- Play helps us adapt, solve problems, and think more creatively.
- Play improves relationships.
- Play can be a state of mind. Play doesn't have to include a specific activity; it can also be a state of mind.
- Developing a playful nature helps you loosen up in stressful situations.
- Playing is fun. Fun is contagious.
- Play promotes mastery, positive emotions, and joy in you.
- Play can heal.
- Play can provide a powerful healing tool that reduces trauma's effects. Play also increases self-worth and vital self-determination.
- Play makes you laugh.
- Play adds meaning to life.

Play means different things to different people. It is important to consider what play means and how you can prioritize joy as a form of self-care. Safeguarding mental health is a prime concern. Life will have ups and downs and will not always be easy. All humans are presented with challenging moments. Play matters and is accessible at any time. Find ways to prioritize some fun, joy and play in your life. It's instrumental for safeguarding mental well-being. Play is a form of self-care.

REFLECTION QUESTION:

- What kinds of play might you enjoy that can also raise your mood?

The Joy of Movement: The Runner's High is an expression that describes a heightened state due to running. A similar bliss can be found in any sustained physical activity, whether hiking, swimming, cycling, dancing, or yoga. It is the brain's way of rewarding you for exercising. In the book The Joy of Movement: How Exercise Helps Us Find Happiness, Hope, Connection, and Courage, Kelly McGonigal, Ph.D., states that it is better to be physical; your brain and body are wired for it. McGonigal reveals that exercise has proven to help you find more happiness, hope, connections, and courage. The joy of movement releases the "don't worry, be happy" neurochemicals. Play and movement are intertwined with basic human pleasures, including self-expression, social connection, and mastery.

Movement doesn't have to be running or an intense fitness class; it can be walking, hiking, mountain biking, swimming, and even dancing. As neurologist Oliver Sacks wrote, "When listening to music, we listen with our muscles." The brain responds to music it enjoys with powerful adrenaline, dopamine, and endorphin rush, which energizes effort and alleviates pain. Music is the energizing force that allows us to feel, express, connect and move.

McGonigal states that movement gives us the perception that: "Whenever I feel that I've reached my limit, I know that there's more in there." It breaks through a phenomenon known as learned helplessness, when you stop trying to improve your situation in other stressful contexts, almost like a defeat response to your challenges. Physical activity and challenge enhance your grit.

Move and Play Outdoors: Spending time in nature isn't just for enjoyment. It's also necessary for your well-being. Many researchers agree that those who play outside are happier, less anxious, and more productive than those who spend more time indoors. Spending time in nature is linked to both cognitive benefits and improvements in mood, mental health, and emotional well-being. Studies also show that being outside in nature is relaxing, reduces our stress and cortisol levels, and decreases muscle tension and heart rates, which are all risk factors for cardiovascular disease.

Natural environments can instill feelings of what researchers call prospect - an elevated perspective and hopefulness, often triggered by natural beauty or awe-inspiring views - and refuge, the sense of being sheltered or protected. Moving in nature is powerful. Science has shown that people who frequently visit natural spaces are more likely to feel that their lives are worthwhile. Movement makes you hopeful! Hope is the elevating feeling we experience when we see a path to a better future in the mind's eye.

REFLECTION QUESTION:

- How do you feel when you are out in nature?

Movement Moves Emotions: The mind and body are intertwined and interconnected. Emotions are felt in the body. Where do you feel emotions in your body? Intense emotional states are often felt deeply within the body. You may say, "I feel a pit in my stomach," or "there's a big hole in my heart." Listening to what the body is saying and honouring emotions in your body will further help process distress. Movement is an excellent release of emotions.

REFLECTION QUESTIONS:

- What form of movement will you add to your life?
- What natural environment can you explore?
- Look for the goal that makes you light up. What is it?
- What have you wished to do for yourself?

LETTING GO TO LIGHTEN UP

Magic of Tidying Up: Decluttering in every aspect has the potential to add more joy to your life. When you lighten up mentally, have fewer decisions to make, and have less stress and fewer distractions, you tend to feel lighter. When you simplify, you have the potential to be more effective, efficient, hopeful, and have fun. Have you heard the expression, "let's keep things light," meaning no drama or baggage? Keeping baggage from the past will leave no room for happiness in the future. Declutter (with yourself or a friend) mentally and physically. Lightening up is a form of self-care.

Tidying and organization spark a tranquil, calm, and motivated space. Letting go is even more important than adding more things to your space and is a form of self-care. You can dramatically transform your life in a single attempt by thoroughly tidying your space. You can let go of the stress of the past and potential anxiety about the future. The question becomes: What do you want to own? What do you want in your life? When looking for stress relievers - make your life simpler and less busy. Clearing and simplifying your environment is a celebration of you taking control of your life. Tidying is an act of balancing. Your living space affects your mind and your body. Be surrounded by things that spark joy and make you happy.

You are determining which items in your living space spark joy and which don't help you clear your clutter. Letting go and tapping into the magic of a tidy house and space brings calm and a motivated mindset that tidiness inspires. Tidying or organizing are often viewed as a chore, but it can feel amazing. Marie Kondo takes tidying to a new level in the book *The Life-Changing Magic of Tidying Up: The Japanese Art of Decluttering and Organizing*. She talks about how a dramatic home reorganization causes changes in lifestyle and perspective. It is transforming. When you put your house in order, you also put your affairs in order. Here are some of her tips.

Use these criteria when tidying your space:

1. Does it spark joy? Choose what you want to keep, not what you want to get rid of. Keep only what speaks to your heart. Discard ALL the rest.

2. One category at a time: Collect everything that falls into the same category, not place or room. For example, choose clothes, books, papers, or mementos.

3. Focus on your stuff: the urge to point out someone else's clutter to tidy up is a sign that you neglect to take care of your own space.

4. Start by discarding. Then organize your space thoroughly, entirely in one go or pick new areas to conquer each time.

FINDING STRENGTH IN STILLNESS

Medical experts agrees that the epidemic of stress is damaging physical and emotional health. In the book *Strength in Stillness: The Power of Transcendental Meditation*, Bob Roth talks about how stress significantly impacts our lives. Stillness and meditation can help to neutralize its buildup. Stress has not always been the enemy. The self-care practice of finding strength in stillness is essential to help you regain your power.

The stress response: The stress response is one of the essential survival tools your bodies have. The fight or flight response is a protective measure activated when we predict potential danger. In the past, if you were to see a bear or a lion or hear a threatening noise, that information would go to the amygdala, the network of nerve cells (or neurons) deep in the brain. The amygdala is the fire alarm that tells your body it is under attack. Two hormones are released when a human is under stress: the chemical messenger cortisol and epinephrine, which flood the bloodstream. If you are already in a high state of stress and anxiety, such as when you experience stress often and repeatedly, you become chronically activated. Stress becomes dis-stress. When you love someone with an addiction, stress is high!

The most important part is how you respond to life stressors. Roth talks about what scientists call your stress response. According to research, stress hits in at least three distinct, often debilitating, ways:

1. In terms of the muscular-skeletal system, you become tense. Tensions affect people differently: tension headaches, stiff neck and shoulders, tight jaw, stomach

digestion, and back pain, which means less oxygen reaches the brain or heart.

2. On cognitive functioning, reduced circulation to the brain skews its electrical activity, taking the brain offline. Stress can shut down the prefrontal cortex, which functions as the brain's Chief Executive Officer or Boss. The prefrontal cortex governs executive functioning: judgement, problem-solving, reasoning, and your sense of self. With the CEO offline, the amygdala takes over the brain's command. With chronic stress, the bottom line is that you chronically act from that fear center where decisions, judgments, and the ability to plan well are reactive.

3. The third component is that your stress response stimulates the adrenal glands to secrete too much cortisol, known as the stress hormone. Stress feeds anxiety, and the adrenals pump out more cortisol, making us even more anxious. Elevated cortisol destroys healthy muscle and bone, slows healing and normal cell regeneration, destroys biochemicals needed to make vital hormones, impairs digestion, metabolism, and mental function, and weakens the immune system. It also affects essential functions such as memory. Cortisol also stimulates your appetite. Finally, it affects

your sleep. Cortisol suppresses your body's melatonin production, which is integral to your sleep cycle.

Two parts of the nervous system keep you balanced: the sympathetic and parasympathetic branches. The rest and digest parasympathetic branch settles us down, while the fight or flight sympathetic branch revs us up. Today, especially with the added stress of loving someone with an addiction, you likely have chronic sympathetic activation and pressure on the body, mind, and relationships.

Balancing the nervous system with mental calm: Relaxation, breathwork, mental stillness, and meditation engage the parasympathetic nervous system. Mental calm is one of the most effective and practical techniques for reducing stress. Meditation and mental stillness lead to open-mindedness and creativity. In the book Resilient, Rick Hanson, Ph.D., teaches how to grow a core of calm and strength. Hanson teaches about the power of mindfulness and how what we focus on is what shapes our brains.

Mindfulness allows you to determine your focus, such as compassion and gratitude. You can use your mind to decrease what is painful and increase what is enjoyable. Humans have three basic needs; safety, satisfaction, and connection. It is essential to avoid harm, approach reward, and attach to others. Mindfulness encourages calm and the responsive neocortex part of the brain to handle challenges and be more resilient. Mindfulness is a form of self-care.

Here are some suggestions for opportunities for mental stillness:

- Slow deep breaths.
- Guided meditations.
- Play calm music.
- Attending to your body (scan and de-stress).
- Listening to all your senses.
- Journal (write it out).
- Yoga.
- Meditate.
- Look at the sky with awe.
- Declutter your space.
- Rhythmic exercise or movement.
- Focus on one thing and stay with it.
- Take space to slow down amygdala hijack.
- Find the positive.
- Daily check-in (What am I feeling? What am I needing? What am I wanting?).
- Repeat peaceful words, thoughts, or visions.
- Be fully present at the moment.
- Go out into nature mindfully.
- Practice, practice, practice mental stillness.

REFLECTION QUESTION:

- How will you implement mental stillness into your life?

NOURISHMENT

Food and adequate sleep provide the nutrients and support for overall health. When the body is well nourished from a balanced diet, proper sleep and hydration, some benefits include a well-functioning immune system. Healthy skin, teeth, and eyes. Strength of muscles and bones. Nourishment provides food, water, and sleep for life, growth, and good health. It's how you treat yourself in every aspect of your life. It's taking exquisite care of yourself. Taking care of yourself at a fundamental level is essential for regaining your power and strength. Slowly start incorporating some of the many ways to nourish your mind, body and soul included in this book into your daily routine and see how they positively impact your overall health.

Eat Nutritiously

Food provides nutrients and support for overall health. When the body is well nourished from a balanced diet, some benefits include

- A well-functioning immune system.
- Healthy skin, teeth, and eyes.
- Strength of muscles and bones.
- It helps you heal.
- Fight illness
- Move well as you age.
- Protect your mental health against the stresses of life.

Nourishment is providing yourself with the necessary food for life, growth, and good health. Eating nourishing food is one of the most basic ways to support physical and mental health. Your bodies use nutrients from food to make the components that carry out hundreds of processes. Eating nutritious foods is crucial to strengthening resilience because well-nourished individuals are healthier, can work harder and have more significant physical reserves. Getting the proper nutrition is the best way to ensure your body has adequate fuel to keep you going. Eating more plant-based foods improves your gut health, so you can better absorb the nutrients from the food that support your immune system and reduce inflammation. Try finding ways to incorporate more vegetables and fruits into your meals.

A well-balanced diet provides all the energy you need to keep active throughout the day. A balanced diet can support a healthy immune system and the repair of damaged cells. It provides the extra energy required to cope with stressful events. Your mind, body and soul are all connected. When one of these factors is off balance, your whole body will feel it on some level. Healthy eating means eating various foods that give you the nutrients you need to maintain your health, feel good, and have energy.

Practice Sleep Hygiene

Healthy sleep habits are an essential part of self-care. Getting enough sleep can help promote a healthy outlook on life, elevate mood and energy levels, and improve concentration and productivity. Resilience is the ability to adapt and move forward in the face of adversity, trauma, or significant sources of stress. It's a valuable trait to help get you through the tough times and bounce back from life's challenges. Sleep boosts our resilience. Adequate sleep can build greater resilience and help you take on life's stresses when they inevitably happen.

During sleep, your brain processes each day's events, forming memories and discarding any unnecessary information that may otherwise clutter your mind. Good sleep is vital for your brain to function correctly and helps you handle your emotions and impulses better. By getting a good night's sleep, you learn and process information more efficiently, and you can find a good balance between emotional reaction and careful decision-making.

The problem is stress tends to affect sleep. Sleep hygiene becomes an essential self-care practice.

Good sleep hygiene is about putting yourself in the best position to sleep well each night. Sleep is an excellent tool for making yourself more resilient. Try some of these sleep hygiene methods:

- Be consistent. Go to bed at the same time each night and get up at the same time each morning, including on the weekends.

- Make sure your bedroom is quiet, dark, relaxing, and at a comfortable temperature.

- Remove electronic devices, such as TVs, computers, and smartphones, from the bedroom.

- Avoid large meals, caffeine, and alcohol before bedtime.

- Get some exercise. Being physically active during the day can help you fall asleep more easily at night.

- Create bedtime rituals to support your sleep process.

REFLECTION QUESTION:

- What sleep hygiene practices will help you sleep?

HOLISTIC SELF-CARE WELLNESS

Self-Care to Enhance Your Physical Health: Sleep. Personal hygiene. Healthy diet. Movement. Walk. Take yourself on a date. Drink water: self-massage or professional massage. Take a bath. Hike in nature. Sauna. Yoga. Tai Chi. Breathe deeply.

Self-Care to Enhance Your Mental Health: Practice relaxation techniques. Be mindful of your own needs. Enjoy nature—practice self-acceptance. Take a nap. Read a book. Learn something new. Self-reflection time. Journal. Write letters of gratitude. Send yourself a love letter.

Self-Care to Enhance Your Social Health: Join support groups. Therapy. Laugh. Be with friends. Call family. Set and practice boundaries. Talk with others. Set up meetings. Join a group or class.

Self-Care to Enhance Your Emotional Health: Journal emotions. Seek pleasure. Experience joy. Listen to music. Let go of responsibility. Have some fun and play.

Plan a 30-Day Self-Care Challenge: Decide what self-care actions or habits you want to create or apply to your life and commit to doing it for 30 days. For the next 30 days, I will...

_____

_____

_____

MAKE SELF-CARE A HABIT

In the book *Atomic Habits: An Easy & Proven Way to Build Good Habits & Break Bad Ones,* James Clear talks about how tiny changes create remarkable results. Minor improvements have shown to accumulate into outstanding results! It is easy to overestimate the importance of one defining moment and underestimate the value of making minor improvements daily. Habit is a powerful way to integrate and prioritize self-care practices.

Habits are the instigators of self-improvement. In the same way, money multiplies through compound interest; the impact of your habits multiplies as you repeat them. Here are some of his tips to implement new habits and get rid of old habits that you don't want or serve you anymore:

Focus on Systems: Instead of focusing on goals, try focusing on the daily systems you put into place. The outcome has little to do with the goal itself but with the day-to-day plans, you implemented.

Ask Yourself: Asking the question, "Are you becoming the type of person you want to become? "What do you need to do regularly to get closer to this person? You choose your identity and reinforce it with habits. Today your habits matter because they form your identity and help you achieve all the things you want to become. You become your habits.

Define Your Habits: The best way to change your behaviour is to make habits that are obvious, attractive, easy, and satisfying! What new habits do you desire for yourself? Are they obvious, attractive, easy, and satisfying? Write them out and start small. Be consistent!

Habit Tracking: Track your daily progress. Make a list of daily actions you'd like to start to get closer to the identity you desire for yourself. If you want more peace in your life, for example, a daily action might meditate at bedtime—track your daily meditations on a calendar.

Consider keystone habits: In the Book *The Power of Habit*, Charles Duhigg talks about keystone habits. These habits automatically lead to multiple positive behaviours and positive effects. Some keystone habits might be: waking up early, having a morning workout, having a morning ritual, meditating, and planning in advance.

REFLECTION QUESTIONS:

- What are your keystone habits?
- What action automatically makes other positive behaviours and positively affects your life?
- Who do you want to be, and what atomic habits will get you closer to that desire?

KEY TAKE-AWAYS

⊘ Self-care is about doing things to enhance your emotional, psychological, spiritual, and physical health. Good self-care is the key to well-being.

⊘ Stress plays a role in the decline of well-being. Self-care becomes essential to regain your power.

⊘ Self-care is critical to maintaining positive feelings; it boosts your confidence and helps you be optimistic about your future. Self-care is also essential to maintain a healthy relationship with yourself.

⊘ Self-care prevents ego depletion and the adverse effects it can cause in our lives.

⊘ Closing the stress loop is a form of self-care and can put you in a position to take better care of yourself and your life.

⊘ Humans are hardwired to take pleasure in the activities, experiences, and mental states that help them survive. Physical activity and play make you happier. Play, joy, and fun are essential to your well-being and the fabric of your life.

CHAPTER REFLECTION QUESTIONS:

Take a moment to write down your highlights from this chapter:

- What takeaways are going to inspire you the most going forward?

_____

_____

_____

_____

_____

_____

- What brought a significant or slight shift in your thinking, feelings, or behaviour?

_____

_____

_____

_____

_____

_____

CHAPTER EIGHT

Your Life Has Purpose and Meaning: Foster Self-Growth, Faith, and Divine Healing

"Not all storms come to disrupt your life; some come to clear your path." — Adage

Self-growth is about understanding yourself and pushing yourself to reach your highest potential. It is a process of being aware of your entire self, having faith in your abilities and taking action to show up and be your best self in this world. Self-development is essential to building self-trust and gives you a sense of accomplishment and meaning. When you develop self-trust, you have more faith in yourself and better understand your life's purpose. Spirituality is recognizing a feeling or belief that something greater than yourself exists and that you are more than just your physical world. By merely growing and opening your heart to the magic that is you, you will bring you a sense of peace, purpose and meaning. Self-growth, faith, and spirituality are critical elements that will help you embrace your power.

Life happens, and challenges will present themselves. Spirituality is one of the most powerful resources at a breaking point or the deepest point in your life. When all else feels hopeless, personal growth, faith and spirituality are available. It is about being grounded in your heart, feeling at peace, and connecting to your innate wisdom. Spirituality is about gaining more clarity and can help you with many aspects of your life. Spirituality and faith enable you to cope, find meaning and move forward with love, hope, and purpose.

In this chapter, you will learn the following:
- What self-growth is and why it is vital for gaining power.
- How to use self-growth for a sense of accomplishment and achievement.
- What spirituality is and how it can support you.
- How to regain your power with faith and self-trust.
- Tools, practices, and rituals to support your growth, faith, and spirituality.

WHAT IS PERSONAL GROWTH?

You often hear the expression make lemonade from lemons, look for the rainbows in the storm, or to search for the silver lining. What exactly is personal growth? Is this positive thinking? In other words, you are taught to look for meaning and possible growth in life circumstances. After all, you have a meaning-making brain which wants to make sense of the world around you. Personal growth is about self-improvement that goes beyond just positive thinking. It's about improving your habits, behaviours, actions, and reactions. Personal growth is an ongoing process. Sometimes, obstacles and difficulties are the triggers that awaken the desire to grow and can lead to profound changes in your life. It's hard to think that something good might come out of loving someone with an addiction, but the struggle can create a new path, expand your knowledge and self-awareness, and even help you grow as a human. Through tough times, you can tap into your spirituality and personal growth.

Personal development and growth is a transformational process that involves improvements in your emotional, intellectual, and spiritual state. Life events, even trauma, can trigger personal growth and meaning that is empowering. Personal growth leads to a more satisfying and meaningful life. Generally, personal growth and development become essential when feeling unsatisfied or unclear about your life's direction.

In the book *Transcend: The New Science of Self-Actualization*, Scott Barry Kaufman, Ph.D., explains spirituality as revealing a new level of human potential and growth that connects you to your highest potential. Kaufman talks about the importance of self-actualization being the art and science of becoming more fully human, in other words, realizing your potential, developing your abilities and an appreciation for life. Self-growth nurtures and enhances a more profound connection with your highest potential and the rest of humanity.

Spirituality and personal growth involve harnessing all that you are while, in turn, realizing you at your best so you can help raise the bar for the whole of humanity.

DAILY LIFE PERSONAL GROWTH STRATEGIES:

- Find inspiration, mentors or role models.
- Read about something you want to develop.
- Form daily habits that will help you grow.
- Find others that will push you.
- Learn something new.

- Wake up earlier.
- Pick up a new hobby.
- Take a new course.
- Overcome your fears.
- Set big goals that stretch you.
- Start something you have meant to start.
- Commit to daily mini-actions.
- Cultivate new habits.
- Find new challenges.
- Prune, sculpt, and clip your life of people who bring you down.
- Meditate.
- Let your hair down, and have fun.
- Stop comparing yourself to others.
- Get out into nature.
- Develop action plans.
- Pursue professional development.
- Grow your network.
- Improve relationships.
- Improve upon your weaknesses
- Create 'to accomplish' lists instead of 'to do.'
- Reach out to new people.
- Exercise and challenge your body physically.
- Journal and plan how you want to live your life to its fullest.
- Get into action.
- Declutter.

- Listen to inspiriting podcasts and books.
- Connect with new people or groups.
- Take a break.
- Make maximum use of your time.

REFLECTION QUESTIONS:

- What does it look and feel like if you imagine yourself at your best?
- How can you start harnessing all that you are?

THE POWER OF REGRET FOR GROWTH

How looking backward can help move you forward. Do you have regrets? Where have you been disappointed in your life? What is regret as a feeling? Regret is a natural reaction to a disappointing event in your life. It could be a choice you made that can't be changed, something you said you couldn't take back. It's one of those feelings you can't seem to shake, a heavy and intrusive negative emotion that can last for minutes, days, years or even a lifetime. But is all regret counter-productive? And can we use it for growth and meaning?

The book, *The Power of Regret* by Daniel Pink changes the typical "no regrets" worldview and helps us realize that regret can be productive or counter-productive, and the best part is that you have a choice. Regret has the potential to be a growth opportunity. Drawing from human psychology, Pink shares actionable steps for transforming emotion into action and using past disappointments to shape purposeful and meaningful futures. Pink teaches that you shouldn't stigmatize regret. You can embrace it. It's a normal emotion and deserves a place in everyone's life. Let's examine the growth potential of regret.

A story of regret: On an April morning in 1888, Alfred Nobel woke up, opened the newspaper, and learned that he'd died. Of course, there'd been a mix-up. Turns out, Alfred's older brother, Ludwig Nobel, was the one who had died. "The Merchant of Death is dead," blared the headline. The obituary then proceeded to condemn Alfred. As you might imagine, Alfred didn't like what he saw. All at once, he was overcome by a very human emotion: regret. Alfred confronted his regret head-on and transformed it into something meaningful. He used it as a catalyst for change. When Alfred did die, his legacy was different. He gave his fortune to create the now-famous series of prizes to those considered to have the most significant benefit to humankind. One prize notably is The

Nobel Peace Prize. Albert Nobel used the power of regret to transform his life for the better.

REFLECTION QUESTIONS:

- How can regret help you improve your life?
- How has regret changed your life for the better?

Unproductive regret: Humans easily get swept away by unproductive regret. Regret is one of the most common human emotions in the world, and humans are meaning-makers, being your brain wants to make sense of the world and make meaning out of situations. Regret can undermine self-trust—the belief in yourself, your abilities and faith in the future. Your brain can revisit the past and invent alternative narratives or fictional storylines that never actually existed. This process is called counterfactual thinking.

To think counterfactually is to imagine how things could have gone or what might have been different "*if only*" you'd done something else. The operative phrase here is "*if only.*" "*If only I'd gotten home five minutes earlier, he would be alive.*" "*If only I listened to the red flags, I wouldn't be in this situation.*"

You are punishing yourself with this flurry of "*if only*" s is fruitless and tormenting. So, instead, taking action in the present to ensure you won't live with even more regret, tormented by "*if only*" thinking, is the best approach. While many people dwell in regret, you can use it to propel you toward a better future.

REFLECTION QUESTION:

- What are your "if only" statements?

The upside of regret: Regret is a valuable emotion. Negative emotions like regret are essential to human growth; denying them is dangerous. In The Power of Regret, Pink talks about your emotions as stocks. Would you invest in only one stock in a financial portfolio? Some emotions are universally considered positive, like love, joy, and awe. Other emotions, like sadness, fear, or regret, are considered much more damaging. Without question, positive emotions should outnumber negative emotions in a healthy mind portfolio. But negative emotions also have their place in your list of investments or lifestyles. Fear shields you from threats like burning buildings or dark alleyways. Disgust prevents you from consuming toxic substances. Then, there's regret, which can help you learn, grow, and achieve your full potential. The emotion of regret is a powerful emotion that can help you.

REFLECTION QUESTION:

- How can you use regret to be helpful in your life?

Make regret a positive catalyst:

STEP 1: Undo it if you can. Perhaps you said something mean-spirited to your significant other. This awareness is the perfect opportunity to "undo" your hurtful action with a sincere apology. Or maybe you estranged yourself from a friend years ago. It's always possible to reconnect.

STEP 2: Is to work on the concept of saying "at least" it _____ . The example in his book was maybe you regret attending medical school, but at least you wound up meeting your spouse there. If there'd been no bad, you'd have missed out on all that good. Analyzing your regrets with a changed perspective can breed appreciation: giving bad experiences a newfound purpose or meaning and making life more profound.

STEP 3: Analyze and strategize; arguably the most crucial step of all since it's the one that promotes growth.

During this step, you could ask yourself: What lessons can I learn from my regret? Recognizing poor choices propels us toward more purposeful, productive futures. Consider finishing this statement after analyzing and strategizing. Moving forward, I'm going to _____ .

Option one, beating yourself up over the past, will only cause distress and disappointment. It's a path that leads to nowhere. On the other hand, these steps offer a much more productive approach to the emotion of regret. There's a big difference between unproductive regret and productive regret. While unproductive regret paralyzes, productive regret catalyzes. And which option you choose is entirely up to you. So the next time you feel regret, pause and ask: What can I learn from this? Use regret as a catalyst for growth, meaning and spirituality. Remember that regret in and of itself isn't a bad thing; it has the potential to be a force of positive change.

REFLECTION QUESTION:

- How can you start strategizing ways to mobilize your regret for better future outcomes?

WHAT ARE SPIRITUALITY AND FAITH?

Spirituality can be seen as becoming more fully human. Spirituality involves recognizing that there is something greater than yourself, something more to being human than just your physical experience. An essential part of spirituality is about opening your heart. Spirituality means cultivating your body, mind, emotions, and energy. It's about expressing your spirit or inner energy and connecting to your divine nature.

Spirituality or awakening makes you more mindful. It is common to go through life on autopilot without giving too much thought to who you are, what you want, or even why you are here. Awakening is about turning on a bright light in a previously dark room. Spirituality also gives us a feeling or sense of connection, meaning, and purpose.

Spirituality teaches you the art of letting go of attachment. Attachments are how you define or label yourself. Spirituality brings about inner peace. It doesn't mean that things in life aren't going to be challenging or that you aren't on an emotional rollercoaster of anger, frustration, and despair. Inner peace allows you to find calm despite the chaos. Spirituality allows you to increase your intuition or connection to energy or source. Lifeforce energy goes up and down. Tapping into the life force through spiritual practices can be therapeutic, support-ive, and healing.

Spirituality increases your ability to be compassionate, mindful, and kind to yourself and others. Spirituality al-lows us to be present and spend less time fretting about the future or regretting the past. Spirituality deepens the mind-body connection, which translates into greater well-being and happiness. A good way of looking at spir-ituality is thinking of it as the spirit, which means it does not belong to the physical, emotional, and mental realms. Spirit transcends those dimensions.

Faith means believing something is true and committing your life to it.

There are two parts to faith, belief and commitment. Faith is the decision to love yourself, no matter the cir-cumstances. And, the more you choose to love, your faith will grow. Hope can't just be wishful thinking but instead based on a hope for a better future for yourself. But how do you keep your faith up even when life is difficult?

Having faith in an underlying order is spirituality. It is about trusting and believing everything intended to be will always find its way. You don't have to suffer, press, or control life. You can influence life but surrender to the natural flow of the universe. Think of spirituality and faith as enlightenment, having knowledge, trust or understanding.

> **Faith is about a belief in yourself and the commitment to take action to support your well-being.**

Consider that you do not have to stagger, limp or struggle through this challenging time, but you can have the attitude of a victor. Faith gives your strength. Psychologists teach that your thinking influences how you feel and behave. As you face challenging circumstances, you become very focused on them. Then these frustrating events could begin to shape your thinking. So instead of allowing yourself to stay there too long, consciously make an effort to focus on possibility and trust. Then you will find that things are possible.

How to build your faith and spirituality:
- Pray and talk with yourself.
- Be generous to yourself and others.
- Meditate on uplifting things.
- Get inspired.
- Connect with others.
- Build self-trust.
- Take good care of yourself.

- Surround yourself with inspiring individuals.
- Decide to have faith.
- Focus on growth.
- Listen to your inner knowing.
- Practice gratitude.
- Learn from the past and keep moving forward.
- Believe in yourself.
- Acknowledge accomplishments and passions.
- Take tiny steps.
- Celebrate wins (big and small).
- Be gracious.

SELF-TRUST TO BUILD FAITH

Faith is about building self-trust. Believing in yourself means having confidence in your abilities and faith that things will work out well for you. It means trusting yourself to do what you say you'll do and feeling that those efforts will result in the desired future outcomes. When you believe in yourself, it starts psychological processes that help you achieve your goals, manifest your dreams, and increase your well-being.

Self-trust breeds faith and hope for a better future for yourself. Faith and self-trust are more than having all the answers or performing perfectly. It has the conviction that you will be kind and respectful to yourself regardless of the outcome of your efforts. That you will have your own back, and things will be okay. It is about relying on yourself at no cost, come what may and faith that you will be okay regardless of what happens.

How to build self-trust

Believe in yourself by cultivating self-empowerment and autonomy. Autonomy is the idea of self-governance. It is the freedom you have to make decisions and pursue unique paths in life. It is also about having faith in yourself and your abilities. Self-trust is self-empowering because it is the ability to take control of your own life, set your own goals, and make your own choices. You can build your self-trust by:

Doing what you say you're going to do. Maybe this means reducing your number of commitments, learning to say "no," or sticking to a schedule. Follow through as often as you can to build self-trust.

Being honest with yourself. Engage in self-reflection to get to the truth of what you think, feel, and need. Try to tune out the "shoulds" of the world to find your true self. Listen to what you feel, need and want.

Doing what you believe is right. Live your values and follow your inner compass. If you're on a path that is true to you, it'll likely be easier to believe in your ability to walk it. Walk your talk and blaze your trail.

Being clear. Get more precise about who you are and what you want. Know what you are willing to do and what you are not. That way, you can trust yourself to make good decisions and perform them effectively.

Renouncing and declaring. Renouncing is to say formally or publicly that you no longer own, support, believe in, or have a connection with someone or something. The meaning of renouncement is to give up, refuse, or resign. Decide what you will no longer tolerate and make a declaration statement.

Shifting your mindset. Develop a growth mindset for learning and growing. Look for and focus on possibilities and options.

Manifesting your desires. Learn the power of manifestation. What you focus on expands. Neurons that fire together wire together. Your brain will notice more of what it focuses on, which is a confirmation bias. When you will look for any evidence to confirm your thinking and find it, is what makes a confirmation bias. You see and confirm what you are thinking. You can use this as a fun, powerful tool to manifest what you desire in your life.

Practicing self-compassion. Know that you have to be your own person and have your own back through times of struggle to build self-trust.

Listen to your needs. Knowing what is important to you and what you value in this life is essential for self-trust—followed by taking action required to meet your requirements or exercise boundaries.

REFLECTION QUESTIONS:

- What does trusting yourself look like for you?
- What are you renouncing?
- What is your declaration statement?

MEANING MAKING FOR DIVINE HEALING

Meaning-making designates the process by which people interpret situations, and events, in the light of their previous knowledge and experience. Meaning-making refers to the processes in which people engage to reduce this discrepancy between stressful events' appraised meaning and beliefs. In other words, meaning-making is the process of how people construe, understand, or make sense of life events, relationships, and the self. How you make meaning out of the circumstances, situations and challenges you go through great impacts your resilience and well-being.

In the book *Man's Search for Meaning* (called initially *Say Yes to Life in Spite of Everything*), Viktor E. Frankl teaches the reader that you cannot avoid suffering based on his experience in death camps during the Holocaust. Still, you can choose how to cope with it, find meaning, and move forward with renewed purpose. Frankl also talks about the importance of love and hope and that love can guide us in the darkest moments. If you have a reason for living and a why, you will find a how. The 'how' can be challenging, as life presents problems and struggles, but the 'why' is a beacon of light in storms. The 'why' gives you a reason to live. Instead of looking at life in terms of what it will or will not bring you, consider why you are here and what you will bring to life. When you lack 'why,' it becomes hard to find hope. You can find meaning in some of the darkest of challenges.

THE UPSIDE OF ADVERSITY

One of the best ways to look at personal growth and faith is to see it as fully realizing your potential. Kaufman talks about the upside of adversity. When the self's structure is shaken, it is best to position yourself to pursue new opportunities. In other words, when you feel the carpet has been pulled out from underneath you, one of the best ways to approach this is through the lens of curiosity, growth, and opportunity. He suggests becoming a cognitive explorer, defined as having a general curiosity about information and options. He recommends viewing everything as growth, even the most challenging of times.

Exploration is about an openness to experience and a focus on growth and the potential to learn, evolve and grow spiritually as humans. You can get energized by the possibility of thinking there is growth. It becomes essential to step back and see the more profound potential of opportunities for growth and meaning in our experiences.

Edward Hoffman and William C. Compton's book *Positive Psychology: The Science of Happiness and Flourishing* talks about how although positive psychology does explore the positive, it also emphasizes the other half of the story. Positive psychology also looks at human suffering, trauma, and environmental stressors. Personal growth is not just about reading positive quotes or messages; it is deeper than that. It explores the dark side as necessary for human development and growth. Challenge, trauma, and struggle to contribute to well-being, meaning, and resilience.

FINDING PURPOSE AND MEANING

Martin Seligman, the father of positive psychology, emphasizes that human suffering and the dark side of life are necessary to enhance well-being. In other words, it's beyond saying positive affirmations, repeating positive quotes, and pretending bad things don't happen. It takes suffering as a starting point or a foundation that allows you to explore transforming suffering into well-being and strengths. Of course, it's not about glorifying suffering but understanding that suffering and challenges in life can contribute to meaning-making.

Real happiness is often birthed from sorrow and suffering, and meaning, strength, and spirituality can stem from grief and despair. The main lessons and psychological research sourced out of Frankl's traumatic experience are

• You always need a reason to live.

- Love goes beyond all suffering.
- Your environment does have an impact on you. However, it can never control your will.
- Your life and everything in it, the good and the bad, has meaning.
- Find a reason to live. Ask yourself: What do you mean to life? What does life expect of you?

Meaning and purpose make you more hopeful for your future. You can turn a breakdown into a spiritual breakthrough and embrace the life-changing magic of spirituality. Psychology researcher George Park offered further advancement in the meaning of life and demonstrated that you could also derive more meaning with:

Comprehension: Making sense of things or comprehending can add meaning. Understanding and creating a sense of coherence in your life enables you to recover from stress or trauma. How can you embrace and accept adversity as an opportunity for growth?

Purpose: Connecting to a purpose, you feel your life is being directed and guided.

Mattering: Feeling like you matter. The degree to which you feel your existence is significant, influential, and valuable to the world.

REFLECTION QUESTIONS:

- How can you make derive meaning from adversity?
- How will you gain greater purpose as you respond to suffering?

STRENGTHS-BASED MEANING-MAKING

Know your Strengths. In the book Strengths-Based Therapy, Elsie Jones-Smith presents highly effective support for knowing your strengths and values. Jones-Smith walks us through strengths-based meaning-making exercises that help you discover your strengths and values. When you take the time to make meaning of challenges and notice your strengths, you are more likely to be hopeful and build faith.

Instructions: By exploring your strengths, this exercise will help you find meaning and value from your own experiences. Strengths-based life stories can help you locate the source of your strengths, utilize them to achieve desired goals, and develop a sense of meaning and fulfillment. During this activity, write your life story in three parts: the past, present, and future. Be creative, but it is essential to emphasize your focus on your **strengths** in each of the three sections. Upon completion, share what you've written with a loved one or friend.

The Past: Write the story of your past. Be sure to describe the challenges you have overcome and the personal strengths that allowed you to do so.

The Present: Describe your life and who you are right now.

- How do you differ from your past self?
- What are your strengths now?
- How have your strengths evolved?
- What challenges are you facing?
- How can you use your strengths to overcome these challenges?

The Future: Write about your ideal future.

- How will your life be different than it is now?
- How can you use your strengths to achieve this perfect future?
- How will your strengths grow?
- What kind of person do you hope to become?
- How will you be different from who you are now?
- What would you like to achieve?
- Finally, how can you go about achieving these things?

By exploring your strengths, how did this exercise help you find meaning and value from your own experiences? What did you take away from this exercise?

REFLECTION QUESTIONS:

- What are your sources of strength?
- How do you use your strengths to achieve your desired goals?
- How do your strengths develop a sense of meaning and fulfillment?

SPIRITUAL PRACTICES

Becoming more spiritual can be a confusing and challenging task, but it is something that you can work on and get closer to every day. Spirituality and faith are nothing you can purchase, a system you can follow, or a program to complete. It is ever-evolving. Spiritual practices could be as simple as reading something inspiring. Keep searching for a spiritual practice until you find what works for you.

Some examples of spiritual practices are:
- Be honest with yourself.
- Be more present.
- Mindfulness.

- Lose the sense of ego or self-focus.
- Forgive people and yourself.
- Enhance your understanding of the world around you.
- Embrace fears.
- Connect with nature.
- Meditate.
- Detach from the material world.
- Breathe deeply.
- Talk to the universe.
- Read something inspiring.
- Pray.
- Attend spiritual services.
- Listen to something inspiring.
- Burn incense.
- Light candles.
- Pull angel cards.
- Journal guidance.
- Practice Yoga.
- Develop rituals for yourself.

THE ART OF YOGA PRACTICE

Yoga is a beautiful spiritual practice where you train your body and mind to be present and aware of your nature. Yoga cultivates awareness, self-regulation, and higher consciousness. Many people practice yoga for their physical bodies and are surprised by its peace and tranquillity. Yoga goes much deeper than physical poses; it is also a spiritual practice. Although yoga is not a religion, this practice has a strong spiritual sense of cultivating self-discovery and spiritual growth. There are many different types of yoga, so be sure to investigate a good fit for your needs.

Some spiritual benefits of practicing yoga:

- Cultivating awareness: You become more aware of your spirit, energy, and internal thoughts. You become more aware of your true self and the essence of who you are.

- Letting go of expectations and control: Yoga is a practice that allows you to develop a spiritual side where you let go of the desire to control and move to a place of surrender and experience without harshness or judgment.

- A quieter mind: Yoga allows you to connect deeper within yourself. You cultivate a calm mind through focused breathing, gentle poses, and meditation. Yoga emphasizes mental focus and clarity.

- Spiritual awakening: You can practice yoga in any faith or religion. Yoga means to yoke or bring together the mind, body, and spirit. This uniting of all aspects of yourself connects you to your higher power and spiritual force. Yoga helps you find peace through love and compassion for yourself and others.

- Emotionally balancing: During yoga and or a meditative practice, you re-focus on breathing and relax the body. Emotional balancing is essential for emotional health when exposed to stressful things.

- Yoga teaches self-compassion and discourages violence: Sometimes you experience self-loathing, doubt, and shame. Yoga prevents you from feeling inadequate and brings about forgiveness, awareness, and truth.

There are many opportunities to get started or restart your yoga practice. How can you integrate yoga into your life?

LUXURIATE IN BREATHING

Deep breathing sends a message to the brain to relax, telling the body to decrease the stress response. Breathing interventions are effective in helping direct conscious attention. Breathing enables you to move into the present moment and calms your nervous system, moving you out of the stress response into a relaxed, joyful calm response. By controlling your attention, you can reach more optimal states of being and thrive at the peak of your abilities.

According to many ancient teachings, breathing generates electromagnetic energy or life force commonly known as Prana, Life Force, Chi, or Qi, deepening our spiritual practices. The breath connects you to your spirit, life force, or energy. Breathwork benefits your mind, body and soul. When you practice, you move beyond your physical body and mind and connect with your spiritual self. You move away from your ego and connect to your true self and the universe.

In the book *A Life Worth Breathing: A Yoga Master's Handbook of Strength, Grace, and Healing*, Max Strom teaches you how mindful breathing, in tandem with the physical practice of yoga and spiritual practice of meditation, raises you to a more robust level of awareness. When you are stressed, disconnected, and anxious, breathing is one of the best practices you can do. Try some age-old breathing practices ideal for stress, insomnia, and anxiety:

Breathing Patterns: Strom suggests the 4-7-8 Breathing Pattern, but you can create variations. If it's bedtime, you can lie in your bed in the dark, ready to sleep. Then, inhale to the count of four, hold your breath to the count of seven, and exhale to the count of eight. He recommends continuing this for two minutes, but you can always do it longer. Essential techniques: Inflate the lungs 100% completely before holding your breath. Always use the same metric and the same numbers. If it's too slow or too fast for you, speed up or slow down your count, but always use 4-7-8. Play with other breathing patterns.

Spirituality Breath: Focus on spirit next time you're practicing breathwork. Feel as though the universe is filling you with air on your inhale. Experience the life force or Prana flowing through you and feeding your cells. Allow yourself to make space for all this energy within you. Feel how this energy is bright, crystal clear, and healing. Feel how this energy connects you to a deeper part of yourself and the universe around you. As you exhale, expand the energy beyond your skin to all living things around you. Visualize a cocoon of white healing light nurturing you.

Pranayama: Pranayama is about controlling your breath for the positive effects that it can bring. You can energize your body, mind, and spirit by managing your breath. You can also use the breath to release tension or energetic blocks that hinder the flow of your life force. Play with your breathing or research pranayama techniques.

Breathing Reminders: Set a timer or alert on your phone to remind you to breathe. When the timer goes off throughout the day, pick one of the following breathing exercises to practice. Pick a different random type of breathing each time the alert goes off. Complete breath/

diaphragmatic breathing: Place one hand on your abdomen and the other on your upper chest. Slowly, and while visualizing the lungs as three chambers, breathe in, filling first your belly, then your chest cavity, and last the top of your lungs (by your collarbone, expanding the shoulders) with air. Exhale and repeat.

Other breathwork inspirations:
- Sigh of relief breath.
- Count Your breath.
- Breath of thanks.
- Breath of fresh air.
- Smelling flowers breath.
- Blow up a balloon breath.

HEALING POWER OF PRAYER

Many studies in the Journal of Experimental Psychology and Psychological Science have found that personal prayer can help people with self-control, forgiveness, and well-being. Prayer is shown to lower anxiety and depression levels and help with the immune system. For many people, prayer is a daily part of life, but many don't realize prayer's positive benefits.

A spiritual life, and in particular, prayer, can be an essential component of psychological well-being. Prayer is sometimes referred to as a direct line to heaven. Prayer is the communication process that allows you to talk to your higher power. You do not have to believe in God for prayer to be effective. You do not need to subscribe to any particular religion or accept any God to meditate or pray. Whether religious or not, praying can enhance your hopefulness, calm your nervous system, and make you feel better. Prayer can be gratitude, confessing, expressing, and asking. Prayer is just like talking to anyone who is supportive, loving, and helpful and is available at any time.

Here are some keys to getting started with prayer or deepening your prayer:

To begin: You can bow, kneel, stand, or walk around when you pray; there are no rules. Choose a position that is going to help you focus. Start by addressing who you are speaking with, be it God, your spirit, the universe, etc., in a way that acknowledges the start of your prayer. You can pray out loud or quietly inside your mind. You can do prayer anytime and anywhere. Commonly, people finish their prayers with gratitude and blessings.

Sounding board: Prayer can be like an imaginary listener who never interrupts you while speaking. This sounding board is also not judgmental and is very understanding. You can even ask questions and quiet your mind to see the response that you receive.

Be honest: Share your innermost thoughts and feelings with no hesitation and complete honesty. It will feel refreshing and liberating to hear yourself speak your truth and listen.

Ask for help: Sometimes, you need additional support and reminders of your strength. Prayer is a beautiful tool and an excellent time to ask for help when needed.

Listen to your heart: Prayer is very compassionate and unbiased. It is a beautiful opportunity to listen deeply without judgment. Listen not only to your heart speaking but also to the answers it provides. Prayer is a lovely way to gain insight and support.

Let go: Praying allows you to process emotions and honour your truth. The idea here is to express your feelings and desires and then let them go. Go with the flow and release expectations or pressure. Prayer generates a sense of hopefulness. Surrender control.

Offer gratitude and appreciation: Prayer is a beautiful opportunity to express gratitude and appreciation for your life and its people.

Guidance: Prayer is also precious for offering advice, direction, and support. When you get quiet in prayer, you can hear your inner voice. Sometimes answers will flow and come to you through prayer. You can ask for what you need and feel supported and guided.

Blessing others: Prayer is a beautiful way to send loving energy to others. The loving-kindness prayer extends health, happiness, and well-being to others.

FORGIVENESS FOR GROWTH AND HEALING

Forgiveness is for you and not for others. When someone you care about hurts you, you can hold on to anger, resentment, and even thoughts of revenge that might bubble up for you. When you love someone with an addiction, the idea of forgiveness initially seems like you are condoning the behaviour that comes with addiction. Not to mention, how do you forgive someone who has hurt you so incredibly? Forgiveness is for your growth and healing; you can embrace forgiveness and move forward.

Who hasn't been hurt by the actions or words of an addicted loved one? Perhaps a spouse has manipulated you, lied to you, let you down or even stolen from you. Or maybe you've had a traumatic experience, such as being physically or emotionally abused by someone close to you. These wounds can leave you with anger and bitterness, even vengeance. Perhaps you feel that, in principle, you have to oppose the injustice caused to you. So, you can get stuck in your suffering. But if you don't practice forgiveness, you might be the one who pays most dearly. By embracing forgiveness, you can also embrace peace, hope, gratitude and joy. Consider forgiveness a practice that can lead you to physical, emotional and spiritual well-being.

What is Forgiveness?

In his book *Forgive For Good*, Dr. Fred Luskin talks about Forgiveness and offers efficient, easy-to-use techniques to lessen the suffering in our lives. According to Dr. Luskin's "Forgiveness," notes the author, "is a complex experience that changes an offended person's spiritual feelings, emotions, thoughts, actions, and self-confidence level. Learning to forgive the hurts and grudges of your life may be an important step to feel more hopeful and spiritually connected and less depressed." Based on scientific research, Dr. Luskin offers startling new insight into forgiveness's healing powers and medical benefits.

Forgiveness is not for another person.
It is for you!

Scientific studies have shown that forgiveness training can reduce depression, increase hopefulness, decrease anger, improve spiritual connection, increase emotional self-confidence, and heal relationships. Pain is unavoidable in life, but suffering? As forgiveness researcher Dr. Luskin puts it, that is another story. Pain caused by other people and the grief that often follows is from our reaction to what others have done. Suffering is workable. Suffering can even be considered optional. Forgiveness is only one response of many you can choose from when you are hurt. Forgiveness is a skill you can learn.

Grievance Stories

Behind much of the pain, suffering, and loss in your life is the story you tell yourself about how you were mistreated. As Luskin cleverly puts it, "you are renting too much space to disappointment." First, you tend to exaggerate how much you have been offended by a parent, friend, boss, or mate. Then you tend to blame everything on this person and nurture your pain over an extended period. By dwelling on your wounds, you give them power over you. Such grievance stories can lead to serious physical, mental, and spiritual problems. The grievance story keeps alive forever.

Many studies show that anger and hostility are harmful to your health and a precursor to depression. You don't want to suffer any more than you have to suffer. You will benefit from realizing you may have a grievance causing suffering. Instead of playing these tapes repeatedly in your head, Luskin recommends you use forgiveness techniques designed to help you take hurt less personally, assume responsibility for how you feel, and become a hero instead of a victim in the story you tell. The funny thing is when you forgive, you don't let the perpetrator off the hook; you let yourself off the hook. Forgiveness is, according to Luskin, one option in a menu of choices you have to respond to the hurt in your life.

Chances are, if you love someone with an addiction, you have a grievance story. Revisit that internal wound. Write down a summary of the experience. Examine what happens when you think about this situation today. Notice how your body reacts when you revisit the hurt. It is likely painful.

REFLECTION QUESTIONS:

- Do you have a grievance?
- How is this grievance contributing to suffering?

Forgiveness training and healing

Forgiveness studies conducted by Dr. Luskin specifically proved that people who completed his forgiveness training reported "a significant decrease in the symptoms of stress." Bad things happen in life. But we don't need to dwell on them. Luskin recommends spending as much time searching out beauty, gratitude, and love in your life as you spend nursing your wounds. He likens this to a remote control that can change channels from the grievance channel to the gratitude, beauty, nature, or love channel. Notice a feeling of peace as you practice this forgiveness training. Try the following suggestions:

Change the channel like a remote control: Switch the proverbial channel from the grievance story to the beauty, gratitude or nature channel.

Use breaths of gratitude: Deep breathing and feeling gratitude for your life.

Take responsibility for your feelings: Notice the good things in your life.

Use positive emotion-refocusing technique: Shift your focus to the good in your life that makes you have positive emotions.

Take hurt less personally: Balance the impersonal aspects of hurt with the person. Recognize when things are not really about you but another person's struggle.

Challenge unenforceable rules: Demanding others to act in the manner you want disrupts your quality of life. Move from should to would like. Anytime you are upset with someone else's actions or something not going your way, you try to enforce an unenforceable rule. Instead, shift to wishing instead of demanding.

Become a hero: Become a hero instead of a victim in your story. Reconnect with your positive intentions and personal goals to change the story you tell yourself. Practice telling a positive intention story.

Write a hope statement: What did you want that didn't happen in a hurtful situation? That can become your hope statement. For example, I hope for a loving relationship with a reliable, honest man with self-regulation that I can depend on.

> *"Forgiveness is the practice of extending your moments of peacefulness. Forgiveness is available anytime, completely under your control. It does not rely on the actions of others; it is a choice you alone can make."* — *Luskin*

So many things that happen to you might seem unforgivable. The pain of personal betrayal by a loved one, a spouse, a trusted friend, or a coworker can seem unforgivable. The act of betrayal causes pain, but the memory of the betrayal often lingers in the form of grudges, painful wounds that never seem to heal, leaving emotional and psychic scarring. Walking yourself through the practice of forgiveness can be a powerful healing journey. The injustices of the past don't have to hurt you today. It all comes back to the meaning you give to your tough times.

YOU, AT YOUR BEST

When you hold the vision of yourself at your best in your mind, you are more likely to succeed. Having a clear vision for yourself can deepen your faith, build self-trust, and add more meaning to your life. I hope you will be who you desire to be and always strive to grow and learn. Taking the time to craft your life vision will help you map a path toward your dreams where you are at your best. Your best possible self means you can imagine yourself in the future when everything has turned out as good as possible for you. Everything has blossomed in this vision, and you have realized your life's desires.

Envisioning your life is flexible, reflective, and forever changing. Taking time to visit yourself at your best allows you to blossom from dreams, hopes, and aspirations. While envisioning yourself at your best, some things to consider:

- Important things to you.
- What are your strengths?
- Where does your passion lie?
- What do you value?
- Who are the kinds of people you enjoy in your life?

Take time to think about your best life and decide on your ideal life. Once you decide that, you can reverse engineer or plan backwards toward your present moment. Are you having trouble? Get inspired by thinking of a time when you were at your best and may have felt productive, successful, and happy, notice details about this event as inspiration and a reminder. Envisioning will reveal your strengths, desires and direction. Now, imagine yourself at your best in the future.

You at Your Best Exercise:

First, take time to quiet your mind and relax. Limit possible distractions.

Begin to visualize yourself at your best in the past. Seeing you at your best in the past will prepare the mind and remind you about your strengths.

Take this time to now shift and imagine your life in the future.

What is the best possible life you can imagine for yourself?

Consider many areas of your life, such as relationships, careers, or health.

Just close your eyes and allow your vision of your best self to unfold.

Imagine a bright future for yourself in which your circumstances change just enough to make your life optimal.

Mentally notice the changes or adjustments that would need to happen.

Be aware of the process it would take to get you to your best possible self.

Consider what action you'd like to put into place immediately.

The more specific and engaged you can be in this exercise, the more you will get out of it.

Once you have painted the picture clearly in your mind, open your eyes and take notes of your thoughts, visions, and ideas in your journal.

Decide what you will implement into your life to get you closer to your dreams and desires.

KEY TAKE-AWAYS

⊘ When all else feels hopeless, personal growth, faith and spirituality are available.

⊘ Personal growth is about self-improvement that goes beyond just positive thinking. It's about improving your habits, behaviours, actions, and reactions. Personal growth is an ongoing process.

⊘ Spirituality can be seen as becoming more fully human. Also, spirituality involves recognizing that there is something greater than yourself. Use it Spirituality to give you a feeling or sense of connection, meaning, and purpose.

- ✓ Regret is a valuable emotion. Negative emotions like regret are essential to human growth; denying them is dangerous.

- ✓ Faith means believing something is true and committing your life to it. There are two parts to faith, belief and commitment. Faith is the decision to love yourself, no matter the circumstances.

- ✓ Self-trust means having confidence in your abilities and keeping faith that circumstances will work well for you. It means trusting yourself to do what you say you'll do and knowing that those efforts will result in the desired future outcomes.

- ✓ One of the best ways to look at personal growth and faith is to see it as fully realizing your potential for becoming everything you are capable of becoming.

- ✓ Real happiness is often birthed from sorrow and suffering, and meaning, strength, and spirituality can stem from grief and despair.

CHAPTER REFLECTION QUESTIONS:

Take a moment to write down your highlights from this chapter:

- What takeaways are going to inspire you the most going forward?

_____

_____

_____

_____

_____

_____

- What brought a significant or slight shift in your thinking, feelings, or behaviour?

_____

_____

_____

_____

_____

_____

MY WISH FOR YOU

*"We can't control the direction of the wind,
but we can adjust our sails." — Adage*

Although it can be extremely taxing and beyond painful, loving someone with an addiction, I know that you can regain your power. I want you to feel your worth, realize your greatness and discover all the beauty you bring to this world. Despite going through loving, or in my case, losing someone with an addiction, I hope you build your resilience and ability to save yourself!

I hope this book has helped you when faced with the hardships that come from loving someone with an addiction to say to yourself, "I see it. I am suffering. And I care about myself." Through the support, you can reveal your human spirit's capacity to persevere and rediscover joy. My goal is that this book offers you an excellent source of loving support while you endure your challenges and know that you are not alone. I also want to remind you that you are worthy of prioritizing your well-being and joyful life.

Loving someone with addiction was one of the biggest struggles I have ever endured. Facing adversity head-on while building my resilience became my lifeline. This book has been my way of turning pain into purpose, and I hope it helps you along this incredible journey back to you, your joy, and your resilience while facing adversity so you can struggle well.

Sending Hugs,
Love Andrea

Please do not hesitate to reach out and join our **SYKM** community.

www.andreaseydel.com
www.savingyouiskillingme.com
www.livelifehappypublishing.com

ABOUT SYKM COMMUNITY

Dear Friends and Supporters,

At SYKM (Saving You Is Killing Me), our mission is to provide compassionate support and valuable resources to those who love someone struggling with addiction. However, we can't achieve this mission alone. We need your help in spreading the word and extending our reach to individuals and communities in need.

Here are a few ways you can help:

Share our resources with support groups: If you're part of a support group for families or individuals affected by addiction, please consider sharing information about SYKM books, podcasts, and the community. Our materials offer insights, understanding, and practical guidance for navigating the challenges of loving someone with addiction. By sharing your thoughts and experiences, you contribute to a community of individuals seeking guidance and inspiration on their own paths to resilience and hope amidst addiction's challenges. Your words may resonate deeply with someone in need of support and understanding.

Inform treatment centers and psychologists: Reach out to local treatment centers and mental health professionals to introduce them to SYKM resources. These professionals play a vital role in supporting individuals in recovery, and our materials can offer valuable support to their client's loved ones.

Spread the word through word-of-mouth: Tell your friends, family, and colleagues about SYKM. Share your personal experiences with our books, podcasts, and community, and encourage others to explore the resources we offer. Your sharing serves as a gift to others, guiding them toward the inspiration and empowerment found within the pages and community of "Saving You Is Killing Me." Thank you for your support in spreading the message of resilience and love.

Make a donation: As a volunteer-based organization, every contribution makes a difference in our ability to continue providing support and resources to those in need. Your donation helps us maintain our website, produce podcasts, and create new materials to support families affected by addiction.

Advocate for inclusive support: Highlight the importance of supporting loved ones of individuals struggling with addiction. While there is significant support available for those in recovery, there remains a gap in support for their families and loved ones. By raising awareness about SYKM, you're advocating for a more inclusive approach to addiction support—one that doesn't cast shame on those who are affected by their loved one's addiction.

Together, we can make a difference in the lives of individuals and families affected by addiction. Thank you for your support and for helping us spread the word about SYKM.

Leave a Review on Amazon: If "Saving You Is Killing Me: Loving Someone with An Addiction" has touched your life, I would be immensely grateful if you could consider leaving an honest review on Amazon or wherever you have purchased this book. Your review holds the power to make a significant difference in helping others discover the transformative journey depicted in this book.

To leave a review on Amazon:
- Visit the book's Amazon page.
- Scroll down to the "Customer Reviews" section.
- Click on the "Write a Customer Review" button.
- Share your honest thoughts and insights about the book.

Explore Our Other Books: Explore our series of books, including "Saving You Is Killing Me: Loving Someone with An Addiction," "Saving Me One Day at a

Time: Finding Light Amidst the Shadows of Addiction," "Tainted Love: A Stay-or-Go Guide to Making Tough Relationship Decisions in the face of Addiction," "Are You Still In There? Understanding Addiction: A Guide for Families and Loved Ones," and the children's book "Sunshine Through The Clouds: A Young Heart's Journey of Resilience Through Family Addiction."

Stay Connected:

Resilience in positive psychology is about more than just weathering life's storms—it's about bouncing back stronger and wiser. At SYKM (Saving You Is Killing Me), we understand the challenges of loving someone with addiction, and we're here to support you on your journey to resilience and well-being.

We're not just a community; we're a family who intimately knows the turmoil of loving someone with addiction. Utilizing the principles of positive psychology and human flourishing, we offer a nurturing environment aimed at enhancing the well-being of our community.

Join our community on social media to stay updated on upcoming events, discussions, and additional resources:

Instagram: @savingyouiskillingme

Facebook Private Group: Saving You Is Killing Me: Loving Someone With An Addiction

Podcast: The Saving You Is Killing Me: Loving Someone with An Addiction Podcast

Website:
www.andreaseydel.com
www.savingyouiskillingme.com

Resources and References:
Visit our website for references, research, resources, and suggested reading to support your journey to resilience and well-being: www.savingyouiskillingme.com

Bounce back, regain your power, and build fortitude using positive psychology. We're here for you every step of the way.

And lastly, if you're curious about putting yourself first, take our MEFIRST Challenge to reclaim your sparkle and prioritize your well-being. Through this complimentary resource, you'll have the opportunity to explore what matters most to you, uncover sources of happiness, and identify growth opportunities in your life. Access it here: www.savingyouiskillingme.com

Remember, you're not alone on this journey. Together, we can empower more individuals to find light amidst the shadows of addiction and create lives filled with hope and resilience. Thank you for being a part of this incredible journey.

Warm regards,

Andrea Seydel

ABOUT THE AUTHOR

Andrea Seydel is a leading expert in the field of positive psychology, holding a degree in psychology with post-graduate training in positive psychology and resilience. With a deep commitment to helping others, Andrea is the founder of "Saving You is Killing Me: Loving Someone with an Addiction." This multifaceted initiative includes a vibrant community, an enlightening podcast, and a series of books dedicated to supporting those who love individuals struggling with addiction.

Beyond her academic qualifications, Andrea has personally navigated the painful journey of loving and losing someone to addiction, giving her a profound understanding of the challenges faced by families in such situations. Her insights into resilience and human flourishing are grounded in both her professional expertise and her lived experiences.

A regular contributor to "Recovery Today" magazine, Andrea is a passionate advocate for those who find themselves in the shadows of addiction. Her dedication to providing support, guidance, and hope to individuals and families impacted by addiction shines through in her work.

For more information and to connect with Andrea, please visit andreaseydel.com or reach out to her directly at savingyouiskillingme.com. Andrea Seydel is committed to helping others find light, strength, and resilience in the face of addiction's challenges.

ABOUT THE PUBLISHER

Dear Reader,

As you hold this remarkable book in your hands, we want to express our heartfelt gratitude for becoming a part of the Live Life Happy Community of readers. Your curiosity and thirst for knowledge fuel our passion for publishing meaningful non-fiction works.

At Live Life Happy Publishing, our mission is rooted in bringing forth literature that not only entertains but uplifts, supports, and nourishes the soul. We firmly believe that books have the power to transform lives, to ignite passions, and to spread joy far and wide.

Behind every word, every chapter, lies the dedication of our authors who pour their hearts and souls into their craft. Their ultimate aim? To touch your life in profound ways, to inspire, and to leave an indelible mark on your journey.

Your role in this journey is invaluable; by sharing your thoughts through reviews, spreading the word to others, or reaching out to the authors themselves, you become an integral part of sparking transformation in countless lives, igniting a ripple effect of joy and enlightenment.

And if, perchance, you or someone you know has dreams of writing, of sharing a message, or of unleashing a powerful story unto the world, know that Live Life Happy Publishing stands ready to guide you. Our doors are open, our ears attuned, and our hearts eager to hear your tale.

So, dear reader, let us, continue to spread the magic of literature, one page at a time. Reach out, share, and most importantly, never underestimate the power of your message to touch lives.

With warmest regards,

LiveLifeHappyPublishing.com

P.S. Remember, books change lives. Whose life will you touch with yours?

Made in the USA
Monee, IL
09 September 2024

65450449R00188